영어 구문의 이해

정 무 주

Hong Ick Publishing Co.

머 리 말

본 교재는 크게 '주요 기본구문 연구'와 '종속절과 등위절'이라는 두 부분으로 나누어서, 영어에 대한 기초지식이 부족한 학생들이 영어 구문을 정확하게 이해할 수 있도록 저술하였다. 소위 수능세대라고 부르는 오늘날의 젊은 세대들은 긴 지문을 읽고 객관식 답을 찾는 데에는 비교적 익숙해져 있다. 그러나 조금만 더 자세히 살펴 보면, 일부 상위층의 학생을 제외한 대다수 학생들은 비교적 쉬운 단어와 평이한 구문으로 구성된 장문의 지문에서 답을 찾는 요령에만 익숙해져 있는 것이지 문장을 정확히 이해하지 못하고 있는 경우가 허다함을 알 수 있다. 심지어는 영어와 한국어의 구조상의 차이점조차 이해하지 못한 채 왼쪽에서 오른쪽으로 차례대로 해석해나가는 학생들을 쉽게 찾아볼 수 있다. 대학 진학을 위해 수능점수에 연연해야 하고, 취업을 위해 토익 점수에 연연해야 하는 학생들에겐 정확한 영어 구문의 이해보다는 객관식의 답을 찾는 요령이 더 필요할 수도 있다. 그러나 영어를 전공하는 학생들은 졸업 후 다양한 분야로 진출하게 될 것이고 따라서 다양한 영어 구사력을 필요로 하게 될 것이다. 빠른 속독도 필요하겠지만 정확한 번역을 필요로 하는 경우도 많을 것이다. 빠른 속독도 정확한 번역도 모두 구문의 정확한 이해에서 나온다는 사실을 아무도 부인할 수 없을 것이다.

본 교재는 이러한 문제점을 해결하기 위하여 제1부 '주요 기본구문 연구'에서는 일곱 가지 주요 구문을 설정하여, 이들이 실생활에서 사용되는 다양한 형태의 예문을 제시함으로써 학생들의 정확한 이해를 돕고자 하였다. 다만 본 교재는 저학년을 대상으로 하는 강의용 교재로 활용할 목적이므로 예문의 수준도 거기에 맞추어 지나치게 복잡하거나 내용이 어려운 예문은 피하고자 하였다. 이러한 일곱 가지 형태의 기본 문형을 바탕으로 하여 2부에서 종속절과 등위절을 다루었다. 다만 2부에서는 종속절과 등위절의 구조 자체를 이해할 수 있도록 하기 위하여 예문보다는 연습문제를 중심으로 하였다.

본 교재가 여러 가지로 미흡한 부분도 많을 것으로 생각되지만, 수업현장의 경험을 살려 학생들의 영어 구문 이해와 더불어 영어학습에 새로운 전기가 될 수 있도록 최선을 다하였음을 밝힌다. 아무쪼록 이 교재를 통하여 영어학습에 새로운 계기가 이루어지기를 희망한다.

2010년 2월 20일

저 자

차　례

제 1 부　주요 기본구문 연구

제1장 주격보어 ······ 14

1. S+V+SC 문형과 연결동사 • 14
2. 연결동사(1): become형 • 16
3. 연결동사(2): remain형 • 18
4. 연결동사(3): 감각동사 • 20
5. 연결동사(4): 외견동사 • 21
6. 연결동사(5): prove형 • 22

제2장 목적격보어 ······ 23

1. S+V+O+OC(명사) • 24
2. S+V+O+OC(형용사) • 26
3. S+V+O+OC(분사) • 29
4. S+V+O+OC(부정사) • 30
5. 지각동사 • 33
6. 사역동사 • 34
7. S+V+O+as+OC • 37
8. 가목적어 구문 • 38

제3장 후치 명사수식어 ······ 39

1. 명사+형용사구 • 40
2. 명사+현재분사 • 42
3. 명사+과거분사 • 44
4. 명사+부정사 • 46
5. 명사+전치사구 • 48
6. 명사+형용사절 • 49
7. 명사+관계부사절 • 50
8. 명사+부사 • 52

제4장 가주어 구문 ········· 53
1. It... to~ • 54
2. It... for~ to~ • 56
3. It... that~ • 58
4. It is said that~ • 60
5. It seems that~ • 61
6. It takes ... to~ • 62

제5장 동격 구문 ········· 63
1. 어(語)동격 구문 • 64
2. 구(句)동격 구문 • 66
3. 절(節)동격 구문 • 67

제6장 강조 구문 ········· 69
1. It's~ that 강조구문 (1) • 70
2. It's~ that 강조구문 (2) • 72
3. It's~ that 강조구문 (3) • 74

제7장 도치 구문 ········· 75
1. 유도부사와 도치 • 76
2. 부사의 강조와 도치 • 77
3. 부정어구의 강조와 도치 • 78
4. 보어의 강조와 도치 • 80

제 2 부 종속절과 등위절

제8장 명사절 ········· 83
1. that-명사절 (1) • 84
2. that-명사절 (2) • 86
3. that-명사절 (3) • 88
4. wh-명사절 • 90
5. whether/if-명사절 • 92

제9장 형용사절 ········ 95

1. 형용사절 • 96
2. 주격 관계대명사 • 98
3. 목적격 관계대명사 • 100
4. 소유격 관계대명사 • 102
5. 관계대명사 what/which • 104
6. 계속적 용법 • 106

제10장 부사절 ········ 109

1. 부사절 • 110
2. 시간부사절 • 111
3. 원인부사절 • 114
4. 조건부사절 • 116
5. 양보부사절 • 118
6. 목적부사절 • 120
7. 결과부사절 • 122

제11장 분사구문 ········ 125

1. 분사구문 전환 • 126
2. 분사구문의 의미 • 130

제12장 등위접속사와 등위절 ········ 135

1. 등위접속사 • 136
2. 상관접속사 • 138
3. 문장의 병렬구조 • 140

부 록

연습문제 정답 ········ 145

제 1 부
주요 기본구문 연구

제 1 장

주격보어

1. S+V+SC 문형과 연결동사
2. 연결동사(1): become형
3. 연결동사(2): remain형
4. 연결동사(3): 감각동사
5. 연결동사(4): 외견동사
6. 연결동사(5): prove형

1 S+V+SC 문형과 연결동사

1. 2형식 구문의 S+V+SC 문형에서 주격보어(SC)는 주어의 속성, 상태, 지위 등을 나타낸다. 이러한 주격보어의 위치에 명사, 형용사, 분사가 올 수 있다.

   (1) Books can become our best friends. (명사)
   (책은 좋은 친구가 될 수 있다)

   (2) Hours after hours the wind became worse. (형용사)
   (시간이 갈수록 바람이 더 심해졌다)

   (3) She stayed sitting on her chair. (분사)
   (그녀는 의자에 앉은 채로 있었다)

2. S+V+SC 문형을 취하는 동사는 주어의 속성이나 상태, 관계, 지위 등을 설명하는 주격보어를 취함으로써, 주어와 보어를 결합시키는 역할을 하므로 연결동사(linking verb)라 한다.

3. be 동사가 가장 대표적인 연결동사이다. 그러나 해석에 있어서 문제가 되는 것은 그 밖의 다른 연결동사가 쓰인 경우이다. 연결동사를 의미에 따라 다음과 같이 분류할 수 있다.

   i) become형: become, get, grow, come, go, fall, run, turn, make, ...
   ii) remain형: remain, stay, keep, hold, ...
   iii) 감각동사: smell, taste, feel, sound
   iv) 외견동사: seem, appear, look
   v) prove형: prove, turn out

EXERCISE 1

1. 다음에서 올바른 것을 하나 고르시오.

1. This tea tastes a bit (strange/strangely).
2. I always feel (happy/happily) when the sun is shining.
3. The children were playing (happy/happily) in the garden.
4. The man became (violent/violently) when the manager of the restaurant asked him to leave.
5. You look (terrible/terribly)! Are you all right?
6. Professor John looked (quick/quickly) at the students' sketches.
7. Our neighbors appeared (relaxed/relaxedly) after their vacation.
8. She felt (bad/badly) about breaking the new watch which my parents had given me for my sixteenth birthday.
9. There's no point in doing a job if you don't do it (proper/properly).

2. 주어진 동사와 형용사를 이용하여 문장을 완성하시오.

feel	smell	*taste*√
look	seem	sound

awful√	fine	interesting
nice	upset	wet

1. I can't eat this. I've just tried it and it *tasted awful.*
2. I wasn't very well yesterday but I ________________ today.
3. What beautiful flowers! They ________________ too.
4. You ________________. Have you been out in the rain?
5. Jim was telling me about his new job. It ________________ quite ________________, much better than his old job.
6. Ann ________________ this morning. Do you know what was wrong?

2 연결동사(1): become형

1. become형 연결동사는 주로 형용사를 주격보어로 취하면서, 원래 동사의 의미와는 관계없이 상태의 변화를 가리키면서 「~가 되다」로 해석하게 된다.

► become, get, grow, come, turn, go, fall, run, ...

(1) At last his dream has come true.
(마침내 그의 꿈이 실현되었다)

(2) This milk turned sour.
(이 우유는 상했다.)

(3) My face turns red when I drink.
(나는 술을 먹으면 얼굴이 빨개진다)

2. 명사를 주격보어로 가지는 경우도 있다.

(4) He turned traitor.
(그는 반역자가 되었다)

(5) This material has gone a nasty color.
(이 재료는 더러운 색으로 변해버렸다)

FURTHER STUDY

1. I take comfort from eating. That's why I am getting fat.
2. Is the earth getting warmer? According to statistics, it is.
3. He didn't know why he was getting so mad at this man he hardly knew.
4. As children get older, the games they play become more complex.

5. You have to rest and eat well when you are studying. Students who study too hard often get sick from exhaustion.

6. In the summer the days grow longer.

7. The fish will go bad if you don't put it in the fridge.

8. At the appearance of Britney Spears, the crowd went mad.

9. Yesterday at the swimming pool everything seemed to go wrong.

10. The weather has turned cold and windy.

11. Bananas turn brown when left outside after a while because certain chemicals in the fruit react with the oxygen in the air.

12. My stomach seems to have doubled in size since I turned forty! I'd better go on a diet.

13. We are running short of gas.

14. The moment he arrived he fell ill.

15. I don't understand it. All day long I feel sleepy and then at night I can't fall asleep.

16. The party came alive when she showed up.

17. However, in the 1970s, there were concerns about the possibilities of nuclear disasters and environmental problems. Then, those concerns came true with the tragedy at Chernobyl.

TIP

take comfort (from) ~을 낙으로 삼다; statistics 통계자료; exhaustion 피로; fridge 냉장고; appearance 출현, 등장; chemicals 화학성분; react with ~와 반응을 일으키다; the moment ~하자마자; show up 나타나다; concern 걱정, 염려; nuclear disaster 핵 참사; tragedy 비극

3 연결동사(2): remain형

1. remain형 연결동사도 주로 형용사를 주격보어로 취하면서, 주어의 상태나 속성이 계속 유지되고 있음을 나타낸다. 따라서 해석은 「~한 상태를 유지하다, ~인 채로 있다」로 하게 된다.

► **remain, stay, keep, ...**

(1) You have to stay calm and patient.
(진정하고 참을성 있게 있어야 한다)

(2) My nose keeps running all day.
(종일 코 물이 나오고 있다)

2. 완전자동사가 주어의 상태를 구체적으로 설명하기 위해 보어를 취하는 경우가 있다.

(3) In my dream, daddy came back alive.
(꿈속에서 아빠가 살아 돌아오셨다.)

FURTHER STUDY

1. Our phone and fax number remain unchanged.
2. You have the right to remain silent and the right to consult a lawyer.
3. Market analysts expect that stock prices will remain steady next week.
4. Visitors to the Center complained that its hours were inconvenient and that it should remain open later on weekend evenings.
5. They can stay alive and grow well only in a certain climate.

6. I don't know if I'll be able to stay awake so late. The 11:00 show doesn't finish until about 2:00 a.m.

7. Many teahouses stay open until 11 p.m. during the week and 2 a.m. or later on the weekends.

8. To stay warm in cold weather, cold-blooded animals must expose themselves to sunlight.

9. Most importantly, you should never panic. Remember to keep calm.

10. He kept silent for 25 years but resurfaced about a year ago sending chilling letters to the police and the media.

11. These measures will help you keep physically fit this winter.

12. Everyone got home safe, and somehow I escaped frostbite.

13. Whom the gods love die young.

14. Most mothers have a good piece of advice: Never go into a supermarket hungry!

15. He spent a year in the hospital, and emerged entirely well.

16. No one was certain if the astronauts who went on these spacecraft would come back alive. But they did.

TIP

consult 상담하다; analyst 분석자; stock price 주가; steady 안정된; inconvenient 불편한; expose … to ~에 노출시키다; resurface 다시 나타나다; chilling 냉기가 스미는, 섬뜩한; measure 조치; fit 건강한: frodstbite 동상; astronaut 우주비행사; spacecraft 우주선

4 연결동사(3): 감각동사

1. smell, taste, feel, sound와 같은 감각동사는 형용사를 주격보어로 취하며, 「(냄새, 맛, 느낌 등이) ~하다」로 해석한다.

   (1) Appetizing food always smells delicious.
   (식욕을 돋우는 음식은 언제나 맛있는 냄새가 난다)

   (2) The soup tastes very good.
   (수프는 맛이 아주 좋다)

2. 명사를 목적어로 취하는 완전 타동사로 사용될 수 있다.

   (3) I smelled the aroma of fresh coffee.
   (나는 갓 끓인 커피의 향내를 맡았다)

FURTHER STUDY

1. But this itself doesn't stink — the bacteria that live on your skin mix with this and can smell bad.

2. The air feels fresher, the flowers smell sweeter, food tastes more delicious, and the stars shine more brilliantly in the night sky.

3. To Mrs. Foster and Miss Rosen the advice sounds wrong, but everyone else at the meeting considers it sound.

4. Most women feel sick in the mornings during the first month of pregnancy.

5. They do their best to create enjoyable and protective environments in which the children feel comfortable and safe.

TIP

stink 악취를 풍기다; brilliantly 찬란히; sound 건전한, 정상적인; pregnancy 임신; comfortable 편안한; protective 보호하는

5 연결동사(4): 외견동사

1. 외견동사란 주로 형용사를 보어로 취하면서, 외형상의 판단을 나타내는 동사로서 「~인 것 같다」, 「~처럼 보인다」로 해석한다. 주어와 보어의 관계를 명확히 하기 위하여 to be를 삽입할 수 있다.
   ▸ seem, appear, look

   (1) He appeared (to be) rich.
   (그는 부자인 것 같다)

FURTHER STUDY

1. The apple appeared perfect, but it was rotten inside.
2. A solid surface may appear perfectly smooth to the unaided eye, but a microscope reveals many peaks and valleys.
3. What's wrong with Jim these days? He seems depressed.
4. The students at a class at Texas Christian University may seem a bit unusual. They are only 4 to 11 months old, but they are students in "Musical Beginnings," a course for parents and infants.
5. Even though they all look alike to us, they know each other by their voices.
6. The lady looked puzzled and her hands were shaking, so Mrs. Baker invited her into her house and gave her some tea. She drank the tea and soon looked relaxed.

TIP
perfect 완전한, 완벽한; rotten 썩은, 부패한; solid 고체의, 단단한; unaided eye 육안(肉眼); reveal 드러내다, 밝히다; depressed 의기소침한; infant 유아; puzzle 당황하게 하다; relaxed 긴장을 푼, 편안한

6 연결동사(5): prove형

1. prove, turn out은 형용사와 명사를 보어로 취하면서 상황의 결과를 가리키므로 「결국 ~임이 드러나다」, 「~으로 판명되다」로 해석한다. 주어와 보어 관계를 명확히 하기 위해 일반적으로 to be를 삽입한다.

   (1) Don't be so nervous, everything will turn out all right.
   (그리 걱정 말게, 모든 것이 잘될 것이니)

   (2) A man who said he can work marvels proved to be a swindler.
   (기적을 일으킬 수 있다고 말한 그 사내는 알고 보니 사기꾼이었다)

FURTHER STUDY

1. The film proved to be too violent for even mature audiences and was rejected by movie theaters across the country.

2. The internet has proven to be a more effective advertising media than television.

3. If any part of the product proves to be defective within two years of the date of purchase, it will be repaired free of charge, or replaced if necessary.

4. The company used a new and innovative marketing strategy which proved to be successful not only in the domestic market, but in the foreign market as well.

5. Yes, it really is. This may turn out to be our most profitable year ever.

TIP

mature 성숙한; reject 거부하다; across the country 전국에 걸쳐; effective 효과적인; advertising media 광고매체; defective 결함이 있는; free of charge 무료로; innovative 혁신적인; strategy 전략; domestic 국내의; profitable 이익이 되는

제 2 장

목적격보어

1. S+V+O+OC(명사)
2. S+V+O+OC(형용사)
3. S+V+O+OC(분사)
4. S+V+O+OC(부정사)
5. S+V+O+as+OC
6. 지각동사
7. 사역동사
8. 가목적어 구문

1 S + V + O + OC(명사)

1. 5형식 구문인 S+V+O+OC 문형의 동사는 그 뒤에 목적어(O)와 목적격보어(OC)를 갖는다. 이러한 5형식 구문의 해석에 있어서 가장 중요한 것은 목적어와 목적격보어의 관계이다. 일반적으로 목적어는 목적격보어의 주어 역할을 하므로, 목적어는 주어로 목적격보어는 술어로 해석한다.

   (1) All the neighbors (S) thought (V) him (O) a hero (OC).
   (모든 이웃사람들은 그가 영웅이라고 생각했다.)

2. 목적격보어(OC)가 명사일 경우 목적어와 동격 관계를 나타낸다. 명사를 목적격보어로 취하는 동사들은 주로 다음과 같으며, consider, believe, think 등은 목적격 보어 앞에 to be를 넣을 수 있다.

   ▸ consider, make, call, think, believe, name, elect, appoint, ...

   (2) I consider them good friends. (them = good friends)
   (그들이 좋은 친구라고 생각해요)

   (3) I believe him (to be) an honest man. (him = an honest man)
   (그가 정직한 사람이라고 생각한다)

   (4) They elected Tom captain of their team. (Tom = captain)
   (그들은 탐을 그 팀의 주장으로 뽑았다)

FURTHER STUDY

1. They consider him an embarrassment.
2. As employees of the top manufacturer of semiconductors, I'm sure you consider yourselves to be experts in your field.
3. The tremendous amount of time spent on newspapers I do not consider reading at all

4. When you are an actor, you must made yourself a different person.

5. He says that just 15 minutes a day is enough to make the world a better place.

6. The great hardness of a diamond makes it one of the most important industrial materials known.

7. When the first white explorers came to the United States, they thought they were in India. That's why they called the native people 'Indians'.

8. Those books which have made a lasting contribution to man's quest for truth, we call great books.

9. People who are old enough to drink alcohol legally are called majors.

10. The greatest boxer in the world was born on January 17, 1942, in Kentucky, USA. His parents named him Cassius Clay, but he is better known as Muhammad Ali.

11. But in ancient Greece, men who wore trousers were thought to be savages.

12. The owner of the newspaper appointed Marcos editor-in-chief.

TIP

embarrassment 당황, 성가신 사람; manufacturer 제조업자; semiconductor 반도체; expert 전문가; tremendous 거대한, 엄청난; explorer 탐험가; native people 원주민; make a contribution to ~에 공헌하다; lasting 영속적인; quest 탐색, 탐구; legally 법률적으로, 합법적으로; major 성인; savage 야만인: editor-in-chief 편집장

2 S+V+O+OC(형용사)

1. 5형식 S+V+O+OC 구문에서 목적어(O)는 주어 역할을 목적격보어(OC)는 술어 역할을 하는데, 목적격보어가 형용사일 경우 목적어의 상태를 나타낸다. 다음 동사들이 주로 형용사를 목적격보어로 갖는다.

► find, consider, make, keep, think, believe, ...

(1) I believe him honest.
(그가 정직하다고 생각한다)

(2) You must keep your teeth clean.
(이를 청결히 해야 한다)

2. 형용사가 목적격보어로 사용될 때, 일어난 동작의 상황을 구체적으로 나타낼 수도 있고, 때로는 일어난 동작의 결과를 나타낼 수 있다.

(3) They catch animals alive.
(그들은 동물들을 산 채로 잡는다.)

(4) Ed pushed the doors open.
(에드는 문을 밀어 열었다)

FURTHER STUDY

1. He found Korean culture similar to Canadian culture.
2. I find all the characters in his new play very amusing.
3. On arriving in England, I found my English quite different from London English. I hardly understood people, and they did not understand me, either.
4. If Rudy had studied German in college, he would not have found the scientific terminology so difficult to understand.

5. The colors are good for the hospital because bright colors <u>make</u> patients <u>happy</u>.

6. Do you believe that the products that you see on commercials can <u>make</u> you <u>happier</u>?

7. People wear jewelry to <u>make</u> themselves <u>more attractive</u>.

8. To <u>make</u> these results <u>statistically valid</u>, we need to question more people.

9. Experts are worried that the economic situation in the United States will <u>make</u> the problem <u>worse</u>.

10. Politicians never <u>consider</u> the opinions of people <u>important</u>.

11. Another problem is that many people do not want to live near wind turbines which they <u>consider</u> <u>unsightly, loud and harmful</u> to birds and other wildlife.

12. Those rich men are great who do not <u>think</u> themselves <u>great</u> because they have money.

13. I have much coffee to <u>keep</u> me <u>awake</u>.

14. A good diet and plenty of exercise will help you to <u>keep</u> your body <u>healthy</u>.

15. In summer it is very essential to <u>keep</u> foods <u>free</u> of bacteria.

16. I advise you to plant more trees in the mountains, because they <u>keep</u> the air <u>cleaner</u>.

17. He <u>kept</u> the matter <u>secret</u> from his family.

18. The ancient Greeks told about Demeter, the goddess of agriculture, who kept the earth green all year.

19. I want everything ready by noon.

20. They set him free on his oath that he would never commit a crime again.

21. Leave me alone, Bill. Mind your own business.

22. You must not leave the door open – the rain will come in.

23. The noise from the construction outside is driving me crazy!

24. I like my coffee hot but not too hot.

25. She painted her eyelids deep blue.

26. All the family were buried alive by a landslide.

27. The hunter shot the wolf dead.

28. 'Good-bye, and thanks!' said Miss Jackson somewhat shortly, pushing open the wet gate.

29. The Trojans, seeing the Greeks leave, flung open the gates of their city and crowded around the great wooden horse.

TIP

character 등장인물; amusing 재미있는; scientific terminology 과학용어; attractive 매력적인; statistically 통계적으로; valid 유효한; 타당한; politician 정치가; unsightly 보기 흉한; wildlife 야생동물; free of ~이 면제된, 없는; plant (식물을) 심다; agriculture 농업; oath 맹세, 서약; commit a crime 죄를 저지르다; construction 건설 공사(작업); eyelid 눈꺼풀; landslide 산사태; shortly 쌀쌀하게, 무뚝뚝하게; fling a door open 문을 왈칵 열다; crowd 몰려들다

3 S + V + O + OC(분사)

1. 현재분사가 목적격보어로 오게 되면 동작의 진행이나 능동관계를 나타낸다.

(1) I am sorry I have kept you waiting.
(자네를 기다리게 해서 미안하네)

2. 과거분사가 목적격보어로 온 경우는 동작의 완료나 수동관계를 나타낸다.

(2) I could not make myself understood.
(나 자신을 이해시킬 수 없었다)

(3) I never heard Spanish spoken.
(스페인어를 말하는 것을 들어 본 적이 없었다)

FURTHER STUDY

1. Once you have gotten through customs, you will find me waiting in the arrival lounge.
2. There I found him lying alone in the back of a cave.
3. When I returned home, I found the window broken and something stolen.
4. I don't want my children associating with drug addicts and alcoholics.
5. Thomas wanted to talk about it, but Susan told him to keep his lip buttoned.
6. Make yourself understood if you are against my decision.

TIP

get through 통과하다; customs 세관; associate with ～와 어울리다; addict 중독자; button (입을) 다물게 하다

4 S+V+O+OC(부정사)

1. 다음 동사들은 목적격보어에 부정사가 와서 「목적어+부정사」의 형태로 사용된다. 이 경우 목적어는 뒤에 오는 부정사의 의미상 주어 역할을 하므로, 목적어를 부정사의 주어로 해석하면 된다.

▶ **advise, allow, ask, believe, cause, enable, encourage, expect, force, order, permit, persuade, tell, want, ...**

(1) I expect to pass the test. (to pass의 주체는 I)

(2) I expect Mary to pass the test. (to pass의 주체는 Mary)
(나는 메어리가 시험에 합격하기를 기대한다)

2. 이들 동사가 수동태로 사용되면 부정사가 바로 뒤에 온다.

(3) My father allowed me to use his car.

(4) I was allowed to use my father's car.

3. 무생물이 주어로 올 때 그대로 해석하면 아주 자연스럽지 못하다. 이럴 경우 주어를 부사적으로 해석하고 목적어를 주어로 해석하면 보다 자연스럽다.

(5) *Her father's sudden death* forced her to give up school.
(아버지의 갑작스러운 죽음으로 인해 그녀는 학업을 포기해야만 했다)

(6) *The heavy rain* caused twenty rivers to flood.
(폭우 때문에 20개의 강이 범람했다)

FURTHER STUDY

1. I didn't want anyone to know about it; it's my secret.

2. Modern cosmology believes the Universe to have come into existence about fifteen billion years ago.

3. Doctors advise parents to give their children healthier snacks such as fruit or juice.

4. Before Mrs. Andrew took the witness stand, her lawyer encouraged her to remain calm.

5. The police have warned the city's inhabitants not to bathe in the polluted river.

6. The policeman ordered the suspect not to remove his hands from the hood of the car.

7. I asked my parents to allow me to study abroad, but at first they wouldn't listen to me.

8. For twelve years, Spanish censorship did not allow Lorca's name to be mentioned or his works to be published.

9. The president didn't know what to say when he was asked to make a speech.

10. Money will enable you to do anything and everything.

11. Sharks cannot see well, but their sense of smell allows them to find food many miles away.

12. Genetic testing allows a pregnant woman to know whether her child will be disabled.

13. Another disadvantage is that TV often causes people to be dissatisfied with their own lives.4

TIP

cosmology 우주론; come into existence 생기다; witness stand 증인석; inhabitant 주민; suspect 용의자; hood (자동차의) 보닛; censorship 검열 (제도); shark 상어; genetic testing 유전자 검사; disabled 불구가 된; disadvantage 불리한 입장

EXERCISE 2

1. 보기와 같이 「목적어+부정사」의 형태로 고치시오.

1. My father said I could use his car.
   My father allowed *me to use his car.* __________
2. Jake says to Peter, 'Be quiet for a minute, Peter.'
   Jake wants ____________________
3. The teacher said to me, 'You may leave early.'
   The teacher permitted ____________________
4. Do you think she'll phone?
   Do you expect ____________________
5. The teacher said to the students, 'Speak slowly and clearly.'
   The teacher encouraged ____________________
6. At first I didn't want to apply for the job but Jill persuaded me.
   Jill persuaded ____________________
7. My advisor said to me, 'You should take Biology 109.'
   My advisor advised ____________________

2. 올바른 동사를 선택하여 보기와 같이 고치시오.

allow√	order	advise	ask

1. The professor said to Alan, 'You may leave early.'
   The professor allowed Alan to leave early.
   Alan was allowed to leave early.
2. The general said to the soldiers, 'Surround the enemy!'
   ____
   ____
3. My friend said to me, 'You should get some automobile insurance.'
   ____
   ____

5 S + V + O + as + OC

1. 목적격보어 앞에 as가 와서 목적어의 자격을 나타내는 동사가 있다. 주로 다음 동사들이 「as + 목적격보어」를 취한다.

► consider, regard, look upon, think of, refer to, describe, designate, ...

(1) They consider it as social equality.
(그들은 그것을 사회적 평등이라고 생각한다)

FURTHER STUDY

1. The biggest difficulty is that people consider smoking as their own business.
2. My stepmother regarded me as an eyesore.
3. She seems to regard any advice from me as interference.
4. Early European settlers used to refer to America as the New World.
5. Children look upon middle-aged persons as extremely old.
6. The founder of our company designated his son as a new CEO.
7. We usually think of history as the story of important people and events, but some historians are also interested in the daily lives of ordinary people.
8. The witness, who had called 911, described the gunman as a white male about 6 feet tall, medium build with fair skin and black hair.

TIP
stepmother 계모; eyesore 눈엣가시; interference 간섭; settler 이주자; extremely 매우, 몹시; founder 설립자; ordinary 보통의; witness 목격자; build 체격

6 지각동사

1. 다음 지각동사 뒤에는 「목적어+원형부정사」 구문이 온다. 이때 목적어는 원형부정사의 주어 역할을 하며, 원형부정사는 동작을 나타낸다. 원형부정사 대신에 현재분사가 큰 의미차이 없이 올 수 있다.

► **feel, hear, see, smell, watch, ...**

(1) I saw my friend run down the street.
(2) I saw my friend running down the street.
(나는 친구가 길을 따라 뛰고 있는 것을 보았다)

2. 진행중인 동작을 지각하였을 경우는 현재분사만이 목적격 보어로 올 수 있다.

(3) I heard a famous opera star sing at the concert last night.
(4) When I walked into the apartment, I heard my roommate singing in the shower.

FURTHER STUDY

1. I see a lot of people riding their bicycles on the sidewalk. Is that legal here?

2. It was a hot day, and the work was hard. I could feel sweat trickle down my back.

3. When I heard the front door slam, I got up to see if someone had come in.

4. I know Uncle Jake is in the bedroom because I can hear him snoring.

TIP
sidewalk 인도; legal 합법적인; sweat 땀; trickle (액체가) 똑똑 떨어지다; slam (문을) 쾅 닫다; snore 코를 골다

7 사역동사

1. 사역동사도 원형부정사를 목적격보어로 취하여 「목적어+원형부정사」 구문을 이루며, 목적어는 원형부정사의 주어 역할을 한다.

▶ make, have, ...

(1) Jane had the waiter bring her some tea.
(제인은 웨이터에게 물을 가져오도록 했다)

2. let, help는 의미상으로는 사역동사가 아니지만 원형부정사를 목적격보어로 가지므로 흔히 사역동사 범주에 포함시킨다. get는 사역의 의미를 가지나 to-부정사가 온다.

(2) My father lets (=allows) me drive his car.
(3) This book helped me (to) see the truth.
(4) Jane got the waiter to bring her some tea.

3. have와 get의 경우, 목적어와 목적격보어가 수동관계이면 원형부정사 대신 과거분사가 와서 「have(get)+목적어+p.p」 구문을 이루며 「~시키다, ~당하다」로 해석한다.

(5) I had my watch repaired.
cf. I got my watch repaired.
(시계를 수선시켰다)

FURTHER STUDY

1. In order to make their dream come true, Mike and Mary decided not to waste money.

2. Last week I was sick with the flu. It made me feel awful. I didn't have enough energy to get out of bed.

3. In the summer, low humidity makes air feel cooler.

4. Please let us know if you require additional information about our products and services.

5. Next, carefully read the information on the package, and don't let words like "New and Improved!" or "All Natural" on the front of a package influence you.

6. Other scientists think that sleep helps the body to grow and to relieve stress.

7. It is difficult to get young people to plan for their old age, which seems very distant to them.

8. Tom had a bad headache yesterday, so he got his twin brother, Tim, to go to class for him. The teacher didn't know the difference.

9. I spilled some tomato sauce on my suit coat. Now I need to get my suit cleaned.

10. If you don't get that furnace repaired before winter, we will freeze to death.

11. The explosions around the world in mobile phone use has some health professionals worried.

12. There is no greater gesture of love than having someone's name tattooed on your body.

TIP

awful 지독한, 끔직한; humidity 습도; additional 추가의; product 상품; package 포장지; influence ~에 영향을 끼치다; relieve (긴장 등을) 풀게 하다; twin 쌍둥이; spill 엎지르다; furnace 난로; freeze to death 얼어죽다; explosion 폭발, 폭발적 증가; tattoo 문신하다

EXERCISE 3

1. 괄호 안의 동사를 활용하여 주어진 문장을 「have + 목적어 + p.p」 구문으로 고치시오.

   1. John's car is running badly. (check)
      John should have his car checked.
   2. Mary's watch isn't going. (repair)
      ____
   3. Mike's trousers are dirty. (clean)
      ____
   4. Peter's hair is getting very long. (cut)
      ____
   5. Helen's kitchen window is broken. (repair)
      ____
   6. Tom and Janet's new car has done 10,000km. (service)
      ____

2. 괄호 안의 동사를 올바른 형태로 고치시오.

   1. Vicky has me (clean) ____________ her car every Sunday.
   2. Vicky has her car (clean) ______________ every Sunday.
   3. I made my son (wash) ______________ the windows before he could go outside to play.
   4. Toshiko had her temperature (take) ______________ in the hospital.
   5. Alice stopped at the service station to have the tank (fill) ______________.
   6. When Scott went shopping, he found a jacket that he really liked. After he had the sleeves (shorten) ______________, it fit him perfectly.
   7. You had better have that tooth (pull out) ______________.

8 가목적어 구문

1. S+V+O+OC 문형에서 목적어가 너무 길 때 그 자리에 it을 가목적어로 두고 뒤로 이동시킬 수 있다. 해석은 진목적어부터 먼저 한 후 목적격 보어를 해석하며 가목적어 it은 해석하지 않는다.

   (1) I make *it* a rule to get up early.
   (일찍 일어나는 것을 규칙으로 삼는다)

2. 진목적어로는 부정사 외에 동명사나 명사절이 올 수 있다.

   (2) You will find *it* pleasant taking a walk with him.
   (그와 산책하는 것이 즐겁다는 것을 알게 될 것이다.)

   (3) I believe *it* true that he cancelled the contract.
   (나는 그가 계약을 취소했다는 것을 사실이라 믿는다)

FURTHER STUDY

1. A: I wish we had a washing machine.
   B: So do I. It would make *it* a lot easier to do our laundry.
2. In an earlier statement, the governor made *it* clear that he opposes taxes on Internet transactions.
3. I took it for granted that he pays for dinner.
4. Despite many years of study, the Korean students still finds *it* difficult to get used to various aspects of American culture.
5. California's soil makes *it* possible for farmers to grow a variety of crops.

TIP
statement 성명서; transaction 상거래; take … for granted ~을 당연하게 여기다; get used to ~에 익숙해지다; aspect 국면; a variety of 여러 가지

제 3 장

후치 명사수식어

1. 명사+형용사구
2. 명사+현재분사
3. 명사+과거분사
4. 명사+부정사
5. 명사+전치사구
6. 명사+관계대명사절
7. 명사+관계부사절
8. 명사+부사

1 명사+형용사구

1. 일반적으로 형용사는 명사 앞에서 수식하나, 형용사구의 경우는 뒤에서 수식하게 된다. 해석은 후치 수식어부터 먼저 한다.

(1) the *city* / notorious for its traffic jam
2) 1)
(교통체증으로 악명 높은 도시)

(2) a simple *diet* / rich in protein
2) 3) 1)
(단백질이 풍부한 소박한 음식)

2. 일부 형용사는 관용적으로 후치 형용사로 사용된다.

(3) the greatest *scholar* / alive
(현존하는 가장 위대한 학자)

FURTHER STUDY

1. Vilcabamba, Ecuador, is another *area* famous for the longevity of its inhabitants.
2. One big *mistake* common to most dog lovers is that they do not try to understand dogs.
3. Doctors recommend that *everyone* older than 6 months receive a flu vaccination before the winter flu season begins.
4. Allergies can remain undetected for a long time because they often cause *symptoms* similar to colds or flu.
5. The Farmers' Club is an organization for *people* involved in agriculture.
6. The *system* in your body responsible for this job is the nervous system.

7. They turn out *goods* comparable to those of foreign nations in both quality and quantity.

8. Late cancellations are subject to a *fee* equal to 50 percent of the cost of the room for one night.

9. The researchers concluded that piano instruction increases children's abstract reasoning ability, a *skill* essential for math and science.

10. If a crisis occurred, *those* unfamiliar with the procedures would not know how to handle the situation.

11. He was a great admirer of the Korean family system, saying that such *virtues* peculiar to the Koreans as modesty and courtesy were the products of the family system.

12. Scientists believe that the people of Hunza enjoy a simple *diet* high in vitamins and nutrition but low in fat, cholesterol, and sugar.

13. Aristotle thought there might be a fifth *substance*, different from the others and somehow more perfect, making up the stars and the universe outside of the earth.

TIP

longevity 장수; flu vaccination 독감 예방접종; undetected 발견되지 않은; symptom 증상; organization 기구, 단체; involved in ~에 관련된, 종사하는; nervous system 신경계통; turn out 생산하다; comparable to 비교할 만한; cancellation 취소; be subject to ~을 겪는; ~할 수밖에 없는; instruction 교육; abstract 추상적인; reasoning ability 추리능력; procedure 절차; virtue 미덕; peculiar to ~에 특유한; modesty 겸손; courtesy 예의; nutrition 영양(분); fat 지방; substance 물질; make up ~을 구성하다

2 명사+현재분사

1. 현재분사가 형용사처럼 명사를 수식할 수 있다. 형용사로 사용되는 현재분사는 진행이나 능동의 의미를 갖는다.

   (1) an escaping *prisoner* (진행)

   (2) frightening *noises* (능동)

2. 현재분사가 단독으로 명사를 수식하면 명사 앞에 오나, 다른 구문을 동반할 경우 명사 뒤에서 수식하게 되며 이를 먼저 해석해야 한다.

   (3) *animals* / growing in natural conditions
   (2) (1)
   (자연상태에서 자라는 동물들)

FURTHER STUDY

1. A new *factory* employing 500 people has just opened in the town.

2. *A ray of light* passing through the center of a thin lens keeps its original direction.

3. Two people were killed and four injured this morning when a *lorry* carrying concrete pipes overturned in the center of Portsmouth and hit two cars.

4. *People* fishing on a lake must wait calmly so as not to scare the fish away.

5. Young *couples* getting married think they will be sitting side by side in rocking chairs in 60 years.

6. The town was destroyed by a hurricane with *winds* reaching speeds of over 100 kilometers an hour.

7. One of the *people* working on the book of the future is Professor Joseph Jacobson from the Massachusetts Institute of Technology in the U.S.

8. When she was 6, her mother asked Renee and her brother, Drew, if they wanted to be in *an art film* being shot in a nearby town.

9. The International Monetary Fund (IMF) said that economic *trouble* affecting Asian countries will begin to get better by the first half of 1999.

10. A *hurricane wind* blowing 100 miles an hour exerts a tremendous force on the vertical *surface* facing the wind.

11. The truth, however, is that it's still more economical to buy a few uniforms than to buy all the different clothes and shoes that a *child* going to a school without uniforms needs.

12. Almost every morning I receive *cards* inviting me to art exhibitions, and on the cards are photographs of the works exhibited.

13. The psychologist spoke to us about some of the amazing coincidences in the lives of *twins* living apart from each other from birth.

TIP

a ray of sunlight 한 줄기의 햇빛; overturn 뒤집히다; so as to ~하기 위하여; scare 겁주어 쫓아버리다; rocking chair 흔들의자; affect ~에 영향을 미치다; exert (힘 · 능력 등을) 발휘하다, 행사하다; tremendous 엄청난; vertical 수직의; economical 경제적인, 절약이 되는; exhibition 전시회; psychologist 심리학자; coincidence 우연의 일치; apart 떨어져서 (from)

3 명사 + 과거분사

1. 과거분사도 형용사처럼 명사를 수식할 수 있다. 형용사로 사용되는 과거분사는 완료나 수동의 의미를 갖는다.

   (1) an escaped *prisoner* (완료)
   (2) frightened *hostages* (수동)

2. 과거분사가 단독으로 명사를 수식하면 명사 앞에 오나, 다른 구문을 동반할 경우 명사 뒤에서 수식하게 되며 이를 먼저 해석해야 한다.

   (3) the *paintings* (2) / stolen (1) from the museum
   (박물관에서 도난 당한 그림들)

FURTHER STUDY

1. The *articles* found in the car helped the police identify the body.
2. *Employees* sent overseas must acclimate themselves to changes in climate as well as diet.
3. The number of *bicycles* improperly parked around stations are increasing, and as a result, a number of bikes have been stolen.
4. Though they take entirely different approaches to the problem, the *conclusions* drawn by the two studies are remarkably consistent.
5. While ethanol can be made from corn, wheat, soy beans, or sugar beets, almost 90% of the *ethanol* produced in the United States is made from corn.
6. The special effects were far more advanced than *those* used in the first Star Wars movie.

7. A trade mark is a *symbol* used to distinguish the products of a company from those of another company.

8. The first item up for bid today is the *trench coat* worn by Humphrey Bogart in the 1942 classic, *Casablanca.*

9. The Hubble Space Telescope can take pictures that are ten times clearer than *any* taken on earth.

10. One of the greatest dancers of all time was a British *woman* named Margot Fonteyn, who danced for over 40 years.

11. A number of beaches in the regions have been polluted by *sewage* pumped into the Irish Sea.

12. The National Academy has issued a 500-page *report* called "Diet, Nutrition and Cancer" that recommends dietary strategies for protecting yourself from cancer.

13. Premature babies who listened to classical music gained more weight, cried less, were healthier, and left the hospital an average of three days earlier than *those* not exposed to classical music.

14. The warning label on *cigarettes* sold in the United States says: "WARNING: Cigarette smoking is dangerous to your health."

TIP

identify 확인하다; overseas 해외로; acclimate 적응하다 improper 부적당한; take an approach 접근하다; remarkably consistent 놀랄 만큼 일치하는; sugar beet 사탕무; advanced 진보된; distinguish … from ~와 구분하다; bid 입찰; trench coat 바바리 코트; sewage 오수, 생활하수; issue 발행하다; recommend 권장하다; dietary strategy 식이요법; premature 조산의; be exposed to ~에 노출되다; warning label 경고 문구

4 명사+부정사

1. 명사 뒤에 부정사가 와서 형용사처럼 명사를 수식하는 경우가 있다. 이것을 부정사의 형용사적 용법이라 하며 먼저 해석해야 한다.

   (1) a *machine* / to do a man's heavy work
   2) 1)
   (인간의 힘든 일을 해주는 기계)

   (2) a new *dress* / to wear to the party
   (파티에 입고 갈 새 드레스)

2. 부정사가 자동사인 경우에는 전치사가 뒤따라야 하며, 명사는 전치사의 목적이 된다.

   (3) a good *house* to live in
   (4) a *chair* to sit on

FURTHER STUDY

1. The first *spacecraft* to visit Mars was Mariner 4 in 1965.
2. The best *way* to recover from one's fatigue is to sleep well.
3. An easy *way* to cut the amount of fat in your diet is to avoid eating red meat.
4. The shop used free gifts as a *bait* to attract new customers.
5. Oberlin College in Ohio was the first *college* in America to accept women.
6. Two years ago, Julia and Brian were single and unhappy in New York. They didn't have *time* to meet a partner because they worked such long hours.

7. He was unable to find the exact *words* <u>to express</u> his sentiments.

8. Susan La Fleshe, the daughter of an Omaha Chief, was born on a reservation in Nebraska. She was the first Native American *woman* <u>to become</u> a doctor.

9. Although he has sought to find a peaceful solution, he is facing *pressure* <u>to use</u> greater military force.

10. Despite the continued *effort* <u>to recycle</u> paper, the amount of wasted paper increased more than 30%.

11. The *capacity* <u>to store and distribute</u> information has increased through the use of computers and other devices.

12. The spacecraft has been silent since it left the earth's orbit last fall on a *mission* <u>to explore</u> comets.

13. *Attempts* must be made <u>to break down</u> the barriers of fear and hostility which divide the two communities.

14. "Energy" and "power" are not the same thing. Energy is the *ability* <u>to do</u> work. Power is the speed, or rate, at which energy is consumed when the work is done.

15. Whether global warming is occurring or not, most agree on the principle of the *need* <u>not to pollute</u> the environment.

TIP

spacecraft 우주선; fatigue 피로; bait 미끼; attract 끌어들이다; reservation 인디언 보호지역; solution 해법; pressure 압력; recycle 재활용하다; capacity 능력, 용량; store 저장하다; distribute 분배하다; orbit 궤도; comet 혜성; barrier 장벽; hostility 적개심; consume 소모하다; principle 원칙

5 명사+전치사구

1. 명사를 뒤에서 수식하는 가장 일반적인 형태 중의 하나가 전치사구로서 이를 먼저 해석해야 한다.

(1) the *books* / on the table
(2) (1)
(테이블 위에 있는 책들)

2. 두 개 이상의 전치사구가 각각 앞의 명사를 수식할 경우 뒤에서부터 차례로 해석하는 것이 자연스럽다.

(2) the *diets* of the *inhabitants* in the three regions

FURTHER STUDY

1. Too much *cholesterol* in a person's blood can cause heart disease.

2. Her *fingerprints* on the gun were conclusive proof of her guilt.

3. No *one* in our office wants to drive to work any more because there are always traffic jams at rush hour.

4. Of the 176 *people* on board, *99* died, including the airplane's pilot, Bob Loft, and the flight engineer, Don Repo.

5. Some were even dressed as *characters* from the earlier *Star Wars* movies!

6. The typical American diet also includes convenience foods, "*junk food*" without much food value, and so on.

TIP
fingerprint 지문; conclusive 결정적인; traffic jam 교통체증; on board 승선한; character 등장인물; typical 전형적인; convenience food 인스턴트 식품

6 명사 + 형용사절

1. who, which, that 등의 관계대명사가 이끄는 관계절은 앞의 명사를 수식하는 형용사절이다. 따라서 형용사절부터 먼저 해석하되 who와 which 등을 '누구'나 '어떤 것' 등으로 해석하지 않는다.

   (1) the British *officer* <u>whom</u> I knew well
   2) 3) 1)
   (내가 잘 알던 영국 장교)

2. 관계대명사는 두 문장을 이어주는 접속사의 역할과 동시에 대명사의 역할을 가지며 선행사에 따라 달라진다. 문장의 25%가 형용사절을 가질 만큼 관계대명사는 독해에서 중요하다.

FURTHER STUDY

1. There are several *places* in the world <u>that</u> are famous for *people* <u>who</u> live a very long time.

2. She believes that *children* <u>who</u> hear music before they are born have "advanced skills in socialization.

3. In Britain, the AA is an *organization* for drivers <u>that</u> provides help when their cars break down.

4. In 1998 Janine Didier was working for an aid organization in Papua New Guinea, a *country* <u>which</u> lies to the north of Australia.

5. Over the centuries, anthropologists have learned, the *clothing* <u>people wore</u> was related to the *position* <u>they held in society</u>.

TIP

advanced 뛰어난; socialization 사회화; break down 고장나다; aid organization 원조 기구; lie ~에 위치하다; anthropologist 인류학자

7 명사+관계부사절

1. 접속사의 기능을 겸한 부사를 관계부사라 하며, when, where, why 등이 있다. 이들이 이끄는 관계부사절은 선행사를 수식하는 형용사적 역할을 한다.

2. when 관계부사절은 시간을, where 관계부사절은 장소를 가리키는 선행사를 수식하는 형용사 역할을 한다. 관계부사 when과 where는 해석할 필요가 없다.

(1) Now is *the time* / when we have to make a decision.
2) 1)
(지금이 우리가 결정을 내려야 할 시간이다)

(2) I recently went back to *the town* / where I was born.
2) 1)
(최근에 내가 태어난 마을로 되돌아갔다)

Further Study

1. Many of us look forward to *sunny days* when we can enjoy a trip to the countryside.

2. Can you suggest *a time* when it will be convenient to meet?

3. I remember *the time* when we couldn't buy bread though we had money.

4. At the *age* when most people retire, he is ready to face a new career.

5. The summer of 1969, *the year* when men first set foot on the moon, we will never forget.

6. Ballet began in Italy about *the time* Columbus discovered America. It was quite different then from what it is.

7. Then *the day* came when I had to go back to school.

8. Perhaps *the day* will come when people will no longer be allowed to drive their cars in cities. This will happen soon if nothing is done to the traffic problem in large cities.

9. The special effects in the movie *Titanic* were amazing. *The scene* where the boat sank was the best one.

10. Technology has advanced to *the point* where a large percentage of the population has personal computers.

11. New Zealand and Germany are *the only countries* in the world where you can bungee jump.

12. *The areas* of the world where people live a very long time are usually near the sea, and the weather is very hot.

13. I have a dream that my four children will one day live in *a nation* where they will not be judged by the color of their skin but by the content of their character.

14. One way of shopping online is through *auction sites*, where people bid for things they want to buy.

15. She learned the value of hard work from her parents. They came from Puerto Rico to *New York*, where Jennifer was born in 1970.

TIP

look forward to 기대하다; convenient 편리한; retire 은퇴하다; career 직업; set foot on ~에 발을 들여놓다; amazing 놀라운; advance 발전하다; character 인격; auction 경매; bid 입찰하다

8 명사+부사

1. 부사는 일반적으로 형용사, 부사, 동사를 수식하나, 명사를 뒤에서 수식할 수 있다.

(1) Do you want *anything* <u>else</u>?
2) 1)
(다른 어떤 것이 필요하나요?

FURTHER STUDY

1. Would you like to go to a movie on Friday night or do you have *something* <u>else</u> to do?

2. The sound of the *radio* <u>upstairs</u> interferes with my work.

3. The products you ordered will be sent to the *address* <u>below</u>.

4. To edit another page, double-click the picture that is on the page you want to work on. Repeat the *steps* <u>above</u>.

5. Drug abuse has long been a major problem for the *authorities* <u>there</u>.

6. The Caucasan diet consists mainly of milk, cheese, vegetables, fruit, and meat; most *people* <u>there</u> drink the local red wine daily.

7. Do you have any recommendations for a good *restaurant* <u>downtown</u> to take my clients for lunch today?

8. After days of searching, the captain found a fine harbor. The *land* <u>nearby</u> had trees and streams.

TIP

interfere with ~을 방해하다; edit 편집하다; abuse 남용; authorities 당국; mainly 주로; recommendation 추천; captain 선장; harbor 항구, 부두

제 4 장

가주어 구문

1. It... to~
2. It... for~ to~
3. It... that~
4. It is said that~
5. It seems that~
6. It takes... to~

1 It... to~

1. 동명사와 부정사는 모두 주어로 사용될 수 있으나, 동명사가 주어로 사용되는 경우가 훨씬 자연스럽다.

   (1) Learning a second language is difficult. (more natural)
   (2) To Learn a second language is difficult.

2. 부정사가 주어로 사용될 때, 그 자리에 가주어 it을 두고 문장의 뒤로 이동시키는 것이 일반적이다. 문장 뒤로 이동한 부정사를 진주어라 하여 먼저 해석하며, 가주어 it은 해석할 필요가 없다.

   (3) It is difficult / to learn a second language.
   (2) (1)
   (제2언어를 배우는 것은 어렵다)

FURTHER STUDY

1. To become a lawyer *it* is necessary to pass the bar examination.
2. *It* is abnormal to have the heart on the right side.
3. So for now, *it*'s wise not to use your mobile phone too often.
4. *It*'s my principle neither to borrow nor to lend money.
5. To load a film into the camera, *it* is only necessary to insert the end of the film into this slot, close the camera, and push this button.
6. In many countries *it* is against the law to discriminate against someone because of their color or religion. Everybody must be treated equally.

7. In the past, some people had slaves. Today *it* is against the law to buy, sell or own another person.

8. I believe that *it* is wrong to judge another person on the basis of race, religion, or sex. I believe all people are equal.

9. *It* can sometimes be difficult to give a verbal description of things like colors and sounds.

10. *It* is still hard to estimate how the recent steep rise in interest rates will affect the stock market in other countries around the world.

11. *It* would be unreasonable to suppose that the books that have meant a great deal to me should be those that will mean a great deal to you.

12. Many economists question whether or not *it* is appropriate to offer this huge responsibility to young consumers who have little or no income.

13. Another reason might be that the process of divorce has become simpler, so one might think *it*'s easier just to get divorced than to work on the marriage.

TIP

bar examination 변호사 시험; abnormal 비정상적인; for now 당분간; load (카메라에) 필름을 넣다; insert 집어넣다; slot 홈, 가늘고 긴 구멍; discriminate 차별하다; verbal description 구두 설명; estimate 평가하다, 추산하다; steep 가파른; interest rate 이자율; affect 영향을 끼치다; stock market 주식시장; unreasonable 이치에 맞지 않는, 불합리한; appropriate 적절한; responsibility 책임, 부담; process 과정, 절차

2 It... for~ to~

1. 「It... to~」 구문의 경우, 부정사의 주어는 일반적인 대상을 가리킨다. 그러나 부정사의 주어를 구체적으로 나타내고자 할 경우, for-구문을 의미상의 주어로 사용하며 이를 먼저 해석한다.

(1) *It* is difficult / for young children to learn a second language.
(3) (1) (2)
(어린 아이들이 제2언어를 배우는 것은 어렵다)

2. 의미상의 주어로 대명사가 올 경우, 대명사의 목적격을 쓴다.

(2) *It* isn't possible / for me to be on time for class if the bus drivers are on strike and I have to walk to class in a rain.

3. 사람의 성격이나 태도를 나타내는 형용사 뒤에서는 의미상의 주어로 of-구문을 쓴다.

► kind, nice, generous, polite, silly, foolish, stupid, mean, ...

(3) It was stupid / of him to give up his job.
(3) (1) (2)
(그가 직장을 그만둔 것은 어리석었다)

FURTHER STUDY

1. *It* should not be possible for us to enjoy our lives without giving something in return.
2. It is very kind of you to give me a ride home.
3. *It*'s illegal for a government official to accept a present in connection with conducting his official duty.
4. *It* is an accepted custom in our country for men to remove their hats when a woman enters the room.

5. We all know that *it* is important <u>for medical directions</u> <u>to be understood</u> clearly.

6. *It* seems difficult <u>for a man</u> who enjoys solitude <u>to like</u> many people.

7. Don't worry Mr. Larson, *it*'s normal <u>for a person</u> who has pain in one foot <u>to lean</u> on the other foot a little more when walking.

8. It needs considerable imagination today to realize how difficult *it* was <u>for anyone</u> interested in music at the beginning of the century <u>to follow up</u> that interest.

TIP

in return 답례로; give a ride 차를 태워주다; illegal 불법의; government official 공무원; in connection with ~와 관련하여; accepted 일반적으로 인정된; direction 사용법; solitude 고독; lean on ~에 의지하다; follow up 계속 이어가다

EXERCISE 4

1. 다음 문장을 보기와 같이 고치시오.

1. Students should do their homework.
→It's important *for students to do their homework.*

2. We don't have to hurry. There's plenty of time.
→It isn't necessary ______________________

3. A child usually can't sit still for a long time.
→It's difficult ______________________

4. My family always eats turkey on Thanksgiving Day.
→It's traditional ______________________

5. Students have to budget their time carefully.
→It's necessary ______________________

3 It... that~

1. 부정사 대신 that-명사절이 진주어로 올 수 있다. that-명사절이 진주어로 오는 경우에도 진주어부터 먼저 해석해야 한다.

   (1) *It* is impossible / that he takes the place of the boss.
   (2) (1)
   (그가 사장 자리를 대신하는 것은 불가능하다)

2. 진주어로 사용되는 명사절의 접속사로서 that 외에 whether와 wh-의문사가 있다.

   (2) *It* is not certain / whether the bus will come or not.
   (버스가 올지 안올지는 확실하지 않다)

   (3) *It* is still a mystery / why he killed himself.
   (그가 왜 자살했는지는 아직 의문이다)

FURTHER STUDY

1. Isn't *it* odd that we three should have met by chance in so large a city as London?

2. *It* was obvious from her childhood that Rachel was a born writer.

3. *It* was Muhammad Ali's belief that the Vietnam War was wrong.

4. Exactly which virus causes the infection is still unknown, but *it*'s certain that these viruses affect children and are highly infectious.

5. *It* is a question why she committed suicide under such a circumstance.

6. *It* is a strange thing how little people really know about themselves.

7. I think we should look after the world. *It*'s important that we don't damage the environment.

8. Is *it* right that famous companies can cut down beautiful forests of trees in South America or use child labor in factories in Asia?

9. *It* suddenly occurred to me that I had an appointment.

10. At this point, *it* suddenly struck me that I was wasting my time.

11. *It* makes no difference what the mayor will say in the interview.

12. *It* doesn't matter whether it's black or white cat as long as it catches a mouse.

13. *It* will not have effects on us whether he will begin the business this fall.

14. *It* occurred to Newton that the force which caused fruit to fall from trees worked quite as well as greater distance from the center of the earth – on top of buildings or even on top of mountains.

TIP

odd 이상한, 뜻밖의; by chance 우연히; obvious 명백한; infection 감염, 전염; highly infectious 아주 전염성이 높은; commit suicide 자살하다; look after 돌보다; damage 손상시키다; make no difference 상관없다; as long as ~하는 한은; have an effect on ~에 영향을 끼치다; appointment 약속

4 It is said that~

1. 「It is said that~」 구문은 다음 (2)의 능동태 구문에서 생성된 수동태 문장으로서, it은 that-명사절을 가리키는 가주어이다. 이때 that 대신에 to-부정사가 올 수 있다.

(1) *It* is said / that he died in India.
(2) (1)
(그는 인도에서 사망했다고 한다)

(2) They say that he died in India.
→ That he died in India is said.

FURTHER STUDY

1. *It* is often said that we do not realize the value of health until we lose it.

2. *It* is thought that computers will play a greater role in the coming age.

3. Millions of people are using cell phones today. In many places *it* is actually considered unusual not to use one.

4. It is generally considered impolite to pick your teeth at the dinner table.

5. *It* has been estimated that about sixty percent of the land at the Badlands National Monument is devoid of vegetation.

6. Today *it* is often reported that among the girls and boys attending elementary school in our country, the number of girls is much smaller than that of boys.

TIP
value 가치; play a role in ~에서 역할을 하다; unusual 별난, 이상한; impolite 무례한; pick one's teeth 이를 쑤시다; devoid of ~이 없는, 결여된

5 It seems that~

1. 이 구문의 it도 형식적인 가주어로서 「~인 것 같다」로 해석하며, 다음 동사들이 비슷한 유형을 취한다.

► **appear, happen, follow, ...**

(1) *It* seems / that he was ill.
(2) (1)

(그는 병을 앓고 있었던 것 같다)

FURTHER STUDY

1. It seems to me that you are not happy about certain words you have to say in this play.

2. As the discussion about their safety continues, it appears that it's best to use mobile phones less often.

3. It appears that a trade war between Japan and China has been averted at the last minute.

4. If it happens that you travel in a foreign country, you will find how inconvenient it is to travel without knowing the native language.

5. If that is true, it follows that he must be innocent.

6. It seemed likely that computers and the internet would replace books.

7. Apartment rental prices have been declining steadily since August, and it is likely that the trend will continue through the end of the year.

TIP

trade war 무역전쟁; avert 피하다; native language 모국어; innocent 결백한; replace 대신하다; decline (물가 등이) 떨어지다, 하락하다; steadily 꾸준히

6 It takes ... to~

1. 「~하는데 시간이 걸리다」란 표현은 take를 사용하여 다음 두 가지 형태의 가주어 구문으로 나타낼 수 있다.

   (1) *It* takes twenty minutes / for me to get to school.
   3) 1) 2)
   (내가 학교에 도착하는 데는 20분이 걸린다)

   (2) *It* takes me twenty minutes / to get to school.

2. 「~하는데 비용이 들다」라고 할 경우, 동사 cost를 이용하여 동일한 표현으로 나타낼 수 있다.

   (3) *It* cost me three days' labor / to finish the job.
   (그 일을 마치는데 3일 걸렸다)

FURTHER STUDY

1. *It* took several seconds for his eyes to adjust to the gloom.
2. *It* takes 365¼ days for the Earth to travel once around the sun. This time lapse is called one year.
3. We estimate *it* will take more than 40 hours to transfer the entire data set from 1.4" diskettes to CD-ROMs.
4. *It* will take two days to enter the data into the computer, and at least a week to analyze it fully.
5. How much would *it* cost to rent a compact car for a week?
6. Many parents complain that *it* costs them a lot of money to send their children to college.

TIP
adjust 적응하다; gloom 어둠; lapse (시간의) 경과, 흐름; transfer 옮기다, 복사하다; analyze 분석하다; compact car 소형차

제 5 장

동격 구문

1. 어(語)동격 구문
2. 구(句)동격 구문
3. 절(節)동격 구문

1 어(語)동격 구문

1. 명사, 대명사를 다른 명사나 대명사와 나란히 놓아 설명을 보충하는 관계를 동격이라 하며, 동격어구 전후에 콤마나 대시(—) 혹은 콜론(:)을 사용하는 경우가 많다.

(1) She decided to audition for a role in *The Mask*, the new Jim Carrey movie.
(짐 캐리의 새 영화, 마스크)

(2) The President of the United States, Richard Nixon, was on television last night.
(미국 대통령, 리차드 닉슨)

2. 동격 표현이 연이어 나타나지 않는 경우도 있으며, 때로는 동격 표현이 세 개 이상일 때도 있다.

(3) An unusual present awaited him, a book on ethics.
(윤리학에 관한 책이라는 색다른 선물)

(4) They returned to their birth place, their place of residence, the country of which they were citizens.
(그들의 고향, 삶의 터전, 자신이 주민이었던 시골)

FURTHER STUDY

1. Sir Geroge Everest, an Englishman, completed a survey of the Himalayas in 1841. Because Everest first fixed the position and altitude of this high mountain, Mt Everest has his name.

2. In 1868, Thomas Edison, surely the greatest and shrewdest inventor who ever lived, patented his first invention.

3. One hot summer day when I was about nine years old, Nancy, the girl who took care of me while my mother was away, took me to the woods near our home.

4. The ancient Egyptians knew that night blindness could be circumvented by eating liver, a source of vitamin A.

5. Actually writing, the most important of all inventions, is relatively new in the long history of mankind.

6. We were witnesses to the old Indian life, the life that had been going on here for thousands of years.

7. The invention of the telephone was the beginning of a few industries that we moderns take for granted.

8. Those seeking a job – the young and the unskilled – realize that the best way to get hired is to acquire some experience from volunteer work.

9. The typical American diet consists of fast foods – hamburgers and french fries. It also includes convenience foods, "junk food" without much food value – candy, potato chips, cereal with lots of sugar but no vitamins – and so on.

10. Science, as we think of it, was born when the Greek philosopher, Thales of Miletus asked a difficult question: What makes up our universe?

TIP

survey 조사, 측량; altitude 고도; shrewd 예민한, 영리한; patent ~의 특허를 얻다; night blindness 야맹증; circumvent 회피하다, 막다; liver 간(肝); acquire 획득하다, 습득하다; volunteer work 자원봉사활동; make up 구성하다

2 구(句)동격 구문

1. 전치사 of가 이끄는 구(句)와 앞의 명사가 동격관계를 이루는 경우이다. 이때 of는 특별히 해석하지 않는다.

   (1) We are traveling around the city of Athens. (아테네 시)
   2) 1)

2. 구(句)동격 구문으로 of+동명사구나 of+명사절이 많이 온다.

   (2) The thought of playing against them arouses all my aggressive instincts. (그들과 맞서 경기한다는 생각)
   2) 1)

FURTHER STUDY

1. A number of doctors believe that taking an aspirin a day can reduce a person's chances of having a heart attack.
2. He was arrested on the suspicion of having accepted a bribe.
3. One of the most serious problems is the problem of how to secure more water for man to use.
4. The summit set a target of halving the number of people without access to clean drinking water from 1.1 billion today to 550 million by 2015.
5. There are many stories of how devoted, and also helpful, a dog was to his master, often saving his life and that of his family.

TIP

reduce 줄이다; suspicion 혐의; bribe 뇌물; summit 정상회담; set a target 목표를 세우다; halve 반으로 줄이다; without access to 접근하지 못하는, 구하지 못하는; devoted 헌신적인

3 절(節)동격 구문

1. that-절이 belief, conclusion, condition, evidence, fear, fact, idea, news, rumor, opinion, saying, thought, truth 등의 추상명사와 동격을 이루게 된다. 접속사 that은 생략할 수 없으며, 해석은 that-절부터 먼저 한다.

   (1) We received <u>the report</u> <u>that she had suddenly fallen ill</u>.
   (2) ... (1)
   (그녀가 갑자기 병들었다는 소식)

2. that-동격절이 연이어 나타나지 않을 수 있다.

   (2) <u>A sudden fear</u> seized her <u>that someone was following her</u>.
   (누군가가 뒤쫓고 있다는 갑작스런 공포감)

FURTHER STUDY

1. <u>The news</u> <u>that</u> her son had been killed was a great shock to her.
2. I'll lend you the book on <u>condition</u> <u>that</u> you will return it within a week.
3. I quite agree to <u>the author's view</u> <u>that</u> a lawyer does not necessarily know all about the law.
4. We can recognize <u>a wide-spread belief</u> among savages <u>that</u> fire is sacred.
5. Do you think there's any truth to <u>the rumor</u> <u>that</u> we're going to be transferred to the West Coast?
6. There is no evidence to support <u>the notion</u> <u>that</u> the more a citizen pays the government, the more he or she gets back.

7. We understand that you are aware of the fact that our insurance company only acknowledges two accidents during the one year contract period.

8. There is increasing evidence that using the Internet opens us up to unwanted attacks.

9. The president assented to the suggestion that his company hire a professional marketing team.

10. But today there is evidence that regular exposure to the ultra violet rays of sunlight, especially if it results in burns, can be harmful to health.

11. The opinion is widely held that knowledge of a language is merely one of many possible roads to the understanding of a people.

12. In writing or speaking English, there is only one general principle that concrete words are better than abstract ones, and that the shortest way of saying anything is always the best.

13. On the principle that if two aspirins are recommended to make them feel better, four will give them even more relief, people exceed the recommended dosage — no more than two tablets every four hours and eight within twenty-four hours.

TIP

not necessarily 반드시 ~할 필요는 없다; savage 야만인; sacred 신성한; transfer 전출시키다; acknowledge 인정하다; contract period 계약기간; assent to ~에 동의하다; exposure 노출; ultra violet ray 자외선; result in ~을 초래하다; concrete 구체적인, 명확한; abstract 추상적인; relief 효과; 구제; exceed 초과하다; recommended dosage 권장 복용량

제 6 장

강조 구문

1. It's~ that 강조구문 (1)
2. It's~ that 강조구문 (2)
3. It's~ that 강조구문 (3)

1 It's~ that 강조구문 (1)

1. 「It's~ that」 구문을 이용하여 강조할 수 있다. 해석은 that-절 부분을 먼저 해석하고 강조하고자 하는 부분을 나중에 해석한다.

   (1) It was Mary that I met in the park yesterday.
   2) 1)
   (어제 공원에서 만났던 사람은 바로 메어리이었다)

2. 주어, 목적어, 부사 등을 강조할 수 있으며, that 대신에 강조 내용에 따라 who, which, where, when 등으로 바꿀 수 있다.

   (2) Verdi wrote *Aida* for the Cairo Opera House in 1871.
   → It was Verdi that (who) wrote *Aida* for the Cairo Opera House in 1871. (주어)
   → It was *Aida* that (which) Verdi wrote for the Cairo Opera House in 1871. (목적어)
   → It was for the Cairo Opera House that (which) Verdi wrote *Aida* in 1871. (부사구)
   → It was in 1871 that (when) Verdi wrote *Aida* for the Cairo Opera House. (부사구)

3. 강조하고자 내용이 주격대명사라도 일상 영어에서는 목적격을 사용하며, that절에 is를 쓴다.

   (3) It's *me* that *is* responsible for the committee.

4. 「It's~ that」을 생략할 경우, 남은 명사가 주어나 목적어에 해당하면 강조구문이고 그렇지 않으면 가주어구문이다.

   (4) It is *you* that are wrong. (강조 구문)
   (5) It is *a pity* that you lost such a chance. (가주어구문)

1. It is often grandmothers who teach children to cook, sew, or knit.

2. And it is the mother who confers with the teacher, attends PTA meetings, arranges for doctor appointments.

3. It is the victims themselves, however, who are responsible for guaranteeing their own safety.

4. 'Were all five people in the car injured in the accident?'
'No, it was only the two passengers who got hurt.'

5. It is the literature which we read with the least effort that can have the easiest influence upon us.

6. Perhaps it is only in childhood that books have any deep influence on our lives.

7. It is only by traveling in, or living in, a country and getting to know its inhabitants and their languages, that one can find out what a country and its people are like.

8. It was my teacher's kind and skillful method of teaching that made the first years of my education so beautiful. It was because she knew the right moment to give me the right knowledge that they were made so pleasant and comfortable to me.

TIP

sew 바느질하다; knit 뜨개질하다; confer 협의하다, 상담하다; PTA(Parent-Teacher Association) 사친회; victim 희생자, 제물; guarantee 보증하다; injured 상처 입은, 부상한; have influence on ~에 영향을 끼치다; comfortable 편안한, 아늑한

2 It's~ that 강조구문 (2)

1. not A but B 구문을 강조할 수 있다. 문장의 복잡성을 피하기 위하여 but B 부분을 문장 뒤로 후치할 수 있다.

(1) It was *not* Jane *but* Mary that I met at the station.
2) 1)
(내가 역에서 만났던 사람은 제인이 아닌 메어리이었다)

(2) It was *not* Jane that I met at the station, *but* Mary.

2. 비슷한 의미의 not A so much as B 구문도 동일한 방법으로 강조할 수 있다.

(3) It was *not* this book *so much as* that one which I bought here
(여기서 구입한 것은 이 책이 아니라 저 책이었다)

FURTHER STUDY

1. It is *not* he *but* you who are responsible for what happened.

2. The child is a natural questioner. It is *not* the number of questions *but* their character that distinguishes him from the adult.

3. An Italian scientist got the idea that it was *not* the bat's eyes *but* their ears that made them able to go about in the dark.

4. It was she, Elizabeth I, *not* her father, King Henry, who led England into the Age of Empire.

5. It is philosophy, *not* science that teaches us the difference between right and wrong and directs us to the good that benefit our nature.

6. All during his political career, Senator Baker believed that it was the nation's welfare that mattered, *not* his.

7. A well-known publisher was recently asked to equip a library in a new house in North London, and the instruction he received was to provide books that would fit the shelves which had been fixed. It was *not* the content of the books that mattered, *but* the size.

8. It is *not just* William's good looks that make people so interested in him, or even the fact that one day he will be King of England. It is *also* because his mother, Princess Diana, was probably the most famous woman in the world.

TIP

bat 박쥐; natural 타고난, 천성적인; distinguish … from ~와 구분하다; direct 이끌다, 향하게 하다; benefit ~의 이익이 되다, ~에게 이롭다; political career 정치생활; senator 상원의원; welfare 복지; equip (~에게 필요한 것을) 갖추어 주다; instruction 지시; fit (치수·목적 등에) 맞추다, 어울리다; shelf 선반

3 It's~ that 강조구문 (3)

1. not~ until은 '~해서야 비로소 ~하다'라는 의미로서, 강조하면 「It's not until~ that ...」 형식이 된다.

   (1) I did*n't* found real happiness *until* I met you.

   → It was *not until* I met you that I found real happiness.
   1) 2)

   (당신을 만나고서야 비로소 진정한 행복을 알았다)

2. 같은 뜻으로 「It's only after~ that ...」 구문이 있다.

   (2) It was *only after* 3 p.m. that he heard the news.
   1) 2)

   (오후 3시가 지나고서야 비로소 그 소식을 들었다)

FURTHER STUDY

1. It is *not until* we fall ill that we fully appreciate our good health.

2. It was *not until* the accident happened that I became aware of my own foolishness.

3. It was *not until* men learned to make things out of metal that they began to take first step in civilization.

4. Very, very early in my boyhood I had acquired the habit of going about alone to amuse myself in my own way, and it was *only after* years, when my age was about twelve, that my mother told me how anxious this singularity in me used to make her.

TIP

appreciate 올바르게 인식하다; metal 금속, 쇠; take a step 한 걸음 내디디다; acquire 얻다, 습득하다; amuse oneself 즐기다; singularity 괴팍함, 기이한 버릇

제 7 장

도치 구문

1. 유도부사와 도치
2. 부사의 강조와 도치
3. 부정어구의 강조와 도치
4. 보어의 강조와 도치

1 유도부사와 도치

1. 유도부사 there는 일반적으로 be-동사와 결합하여 도치구문을 이룬다. 이때 주어는 be-동사 다음에 나오는 명사이며, there는 특별히 해석할 필요가 없다.

   (1) *There* was a good film on TV last night.
   (어제 밤 TV에 좋은 영화가 있었다)

2. 유도부사 there는 be-동사 이외의 다른 동사와도 흔히 결합하여 도치구문을 이루며 마찬가지로 해석은 할 필요 없다.

   (2) *There* came a huge wave.
   (거대한 파도가 왔다)

FURTHER STUDY

1. *There* seems to be so much work to be done this year.

2. *There* have been five accidents at this intersection in the last 12 months.

3. On Mars *there* are mountains that are three times as high as Mount Everest, and canyons that are three times as deep and five times as long as the Grand Canyon!

4. A heavy step was heard upon the stairs, and an instant later *there* entered a tall, ruddy, clean-shaven gentleman.

5. Since the dawn of history *there* has existed in the minds of men the longing for national independence and for individual freedom.

TIP
intersection 교차로; canyon 협곡; ruddy 불그스레한, 혈색이 좋은; dawn 새벽, 여명; longing 동경, 갈망; national independence 국가의 독립

2 부사의 강조와 도치

1. 장소나 방향을 나타내는 부사적 표현을 강조하기 위해 문장 앞에 가지고 왔을 때 주어와 동사가 도치될 수 있다.

(1) A great castle stood on a hill in front of them.
→ *On a hill in front of them* stood a great castle.

2. 정도나 양태를 나타내는 부사적 표현이 문장 앞에서 강조될 때도 주어와 동사가 도치될 수 있다.

(2) He fulfilled the duties so well.
→ *So well* did he fulfill the duties.

FURTHER STUDY

1. *Round the corner* walked a large policeman.

2. Next to the desert floor, the air was hot. *Above this hot air* was another layer of cooler, more dense air.

3. On April 10, 1912, the Titanic left England on its first voyage. *On the ship* were more than 2,200 passengers and crew.

4. Almost every morning I receive cards inviting me to art exhibitions, and *on the cards* are photographs of the works exhibited.

5. *Within the Alamo* were one hundred and eighty men, more than two thirds of whom had recently migrated from nearby states.

TIP
layer 층; dense 자욱한, 짙은; voyage 항해; crew 승무원; art exhibition 미술 전시회; migrate 이주하다

3 부정어구의 강조와 도치

1. 부정어구를 강조하기 위해 문장 앞으로 가지고 올 경우, 주어와 동사는 도치된다.

(1) I didn't say a single word to them.
→ *Not* a single word did I say to them.

(2) I have never seen such a beautiful girl.
→ *Never* have I seen such a beautiful girl.

2. only도 간접적인 의미에서 부정의 뜻을 가지고 있으므로 문두로 오게 되면 도치구문이 된다.

(3) *Only* after a long argument did he agree with us.
(오랜 논쟁 끝에서야 비로소 그는 우리 생각에 동의했다)

FURTHER STUDY

1. *Not* a word did he say because he didn't know what to say in such a case.
2. Under *no* circumstances can we accept checks.
3. *Little* did I imagine that he would make such a mistake.
4. *Seldom* had I seen such a remarkable creature.
5. *Never* in my life have I been so strongly and immediately attracted to any man, before or since.
6. *Nowhere* in the world can travelers buy so much beauty for so little money as in Hawaii.
7. *Not only* did we lose all our money, but we also came close to losing our lives.

8. Although these discount Clothing Stores aren't very attractive, *not only* are the prices low, but you can often find the same famous brands that you find in high-priced department stores.

9. *Only* then did I understand what she meant.

10. *Only* after a year did I begin to see the results of my work.

11. *Only* after it became dark did they take a rest.

12. *Not* until the first land plants developed did land animals appear

13. Not until the 1930's, when the value of sorghum as grain, forage, and silage for livestock feeding was recognized, did its acreage begin to increase.

14. *Hardly* had I arrived *when* I had a new problem to cope with.

15. *Scarcely* had we started lunch *when* the doorbell rang.

16. *No sooner* had his luggage been loaded *than* the jeep started off.

17. I made up my mind to walk all the way home, but I was tired and hungry. To make matters worse, I had *scarcely* started *before* it began to rain.

TIP

circumstance 상황; check 수표; remarkable 주목할 만한, 놀랄 만한; immediately 곧, 즉각; come close to 하마터면 ~할 뻔하다; sorghum 사탕수수; grain 곡물; forage 마초, (마소의) 먹이; silage (신선하게 저장된) 목초; livestock feeding 가축 사육; acreage 면적; cope with 대처하다, 처리하다; to make matters worse 설상가상으로

4 보어의 강조와 도치

1. 보어를 강조하고자 문장 앞에 가지고 오면, 주어와 동사는 반드시 도치된다.

   (1) *Great* was his joy when he passed the exam.

2. 주어가 길고 동사가 be 동사일 때, 보어가 문두에 오면서 주어와 동사가 도치될 수 있다.

   (2) *Even more important* is the fact that television brings the family together in the evening.

FURTHER STUDY

1. *Even more basic* is the eradication of false ideas and unsound way of thinking.

2. Yet criticism does little good. *Especially harmful* is the criticism that is spoken behind the back of the person concerned.

3. *Fortunate* is the man who, at the right moment, meets the right friend: fortunate also the man who at the right moment meets the right enemy.

4. *Contributing to* the increase in food prices from November were some kinds of beef, fresh vegetables, some bakery and dairy products, and sugar.

5. *Related to* the avoidance of excesses is the avoidance of those foods which are harmful to the body. *Included here* are habit-forming drugs of all sorts, such as cocaine, morphine, and marijuana.

TIP

eradication 근절; criticism 비판; do good 도움이 되다; contribute to ~의 원인이 되다; dairy product 유제품; excess 지나침, 과도; habit-forming 습관성

제 2 부
종속절과 등위절

제 8 장

명사절

1. that-명사절 (1)
2. that-명사절 (2)
3. that-명사절 (3)
4. wh-명사절
5. whether/if-명사절

1 that-명사절 (1)

1. that-명사절이 주어로 사용될 수 있으나, 가주어 it와 더불어 문장 뒤로 이동하는 것이 일반적이다. 접속사 that은 생략하지 않는다.

   (1) That the world is round is a fact.
   → It is a fact that the world is round. (more natural)

2. that-명사절이 동사의 목적어로 사용될 수 있으며, 이 경우 that는 생략할 수 있다.

   (2) Even children know (that) the world is round.

3. that-명사절이 전치사의 목적어로 사용될 때는 the fact that 형태로 사용된다. 전치사 뒤에 that-절을 바로 쓰면 어색하다.

   (3) In spite of the fact that Ann was not injured, she was sent to a hospital.

4. be-동사 뒤에서 보어로 쓰인다. 보어절을 이끄는 접속사 that은 생략할 수 없다.

   (4) The first reason is that I don't have enough money.

FURTHER STUDY

1. Copernicus believed that the sun, rather than the Earth, was at the center of the universe and that the planets revolved around it.
2. The fact that everybody liked it once doesn't always guarantee that everybody will like it again.
3. I like her except for the fact that she is over nice.

EXERCISE 5

1. 각 문장에서 명사절이 시작하는 적절한 자리에 that를 넣으시오.

   1. Do you know India has the second largest population in the world?
   2. I hope you'll have a wonderful time.
   3. Don't throw that plastic bag into the sea! Don't you know plastic trash kills thousands of marine animals every year.
   4. I have a test tomorrow. I suppose I should study tonight. but I'd rather go to a movie.
   5. It's hard to deny pollution diminish the quality of our lives.
   6. World hunger is a serious problem. Do you realize more than half of the people in the world go hungry every day?
   7. Right now I'm single. I can't predict my future exactly, but I assume I will get married someday.
   8. The critics praised the movie for the acting, writing and direction, but said they do not believe it will win any major awards.

2. 밑줄 친 부분을 어법에 맞게 고치시오.

   1. <u>Smoking can cause cancer</u> is obvious.
   2. <u>That</u> is a well-known fact that sports are good for children.
   3. <u>The fact</u> we lack clean water is too shocking.
   4. The fact that penguins are good parents <u>are</u> interesting.
   5. I know <u>it is that</u> there are nine planets in the solar system.
   6. The main thing <u>is you</u> are happy.
   7. Parents are responsible <u>for the fact which</u> the children are unhappy at home.
   8. I agree with <u>the view women</u> can be better politicians than men.

2 that-명사절 (2)

1. 다음의 be+형용사 뒤에 that-명사절이 올 수 있다. 일상 영어에서는 접속사 that를 생략한다.

be afraid that	be amazed that	be aware that
be certain that	be disappointed that	be glad that
be happy that	be pleased that	be sorry that
be sure that	be surprised that	be worry that

(1) I'm sure (that) you'll get a good job.

(2) I'm afraid (that) you have the wrong number.

2. 두 문장의 주어가 같을 때 to-부정사로 바꿀 수 있다.

(3) *She* was amazed that *she* found her husband seriously wounded.

→ She was amazed to find her husband seriously wounded.

3. be afraid, believe, guess, hope, think 등의 경우, that-절의 내용을 반복하는 대신 so를 쓴다.

(4) A: Are we going to have a test in grammar tomorrow?
B: I think so.

4. 부정의 경우 두 가지로 나타낸다. think, expect는 「부정문+so」를 쓰고, be afraid, guess, hope는 「긍정문+not」를 쓴다.

(5) A: Is Jack going to water in the garden?
B: I don't think so.

(6) A: Is it going to be cold tomorrow?
B: I hope not.

EXERCISE 6

1. 다음 대화를 읽고 적절한 곳에 that를 넣으시오.

   1. A: Are you sure you'll be on time tomorrow?
      B: Yes, I'm certain I'll be on time tomorrow. It's a picnic day.
   2. A: Are you happy the weather is nice today?
      B: I'm lucky it's a sunny day because today is my wedding day.

2. 각 대화에 나오는 so와 not의 의미를 풀어서 that-절로 바꾸시오.

   1. A: Did you pass the final test?
      B: I hope so. → I hope *(that) I'll pass the final test.*
   2. A: Do you think strong laws are needed to protect the environment?
      B: I think so. → ______________________
   3. A: Will Korea be reunited in the near future?
      B: I hope so. → ______________________
   4. A: Do you think we'll have a math test tomorrow?
      B: I hope not. → ______________________
   5. A: Is there any life on other planets?
      B: I don't think so. → ______________________

3. 밑줄 친 부분을 어법에 맞게 고치시오.

   1. I'm sure <u>because</u> you'll become a good doctor.
   2. "Is it going to rain before long?" "I think <u>that</u>."
   3. "Can you get a job?" "I hope <u>it</u>."
   4. "Can Kevin pass the exam?" "I <u>think not</u>."
   5. "Will it be cold tomorrow?" "I <u>don't hope so</u>."

3 that-명사절 (3)

1. 「요구, 제안, 충고, 명령」 등을 가리키는 다음 동사의 목적어로 사용되는 that-명사절에는 동사 원형이 오며 that는 생략할 수 없다.

advise	demand	insist	order
propose	recommend	require	suggest

(1) The teacher *demands* that we *be* on time.

2. 「요구, 제안, 충고, 명령」 등을 가리키는 다음 형용사 뒤의 that-명사절에도 동사 원형이 온다.

essential	important	necessary	obligatory
urgent			

(2) It was *urgent* that she *leave* at once.

3. 「요구, 제안, 충고, 명령」 등을 가리키는 다음 명사 뒤의 that-명사절에도 동사 원형이 온다.

advice	demand	order	recommendation
request	suggestion		

(3) *The suggestion* that he *be* promoted was with resistance.

FURTHER STUDY

1. The law I am referring to *requires* that everyone *have* his car checked at least once a year.

2. In this country it *is required* that any one who has recently come here *have to* pay taxes.

3. The judge assented to *the suggestion* that the prisoner *be* sentenced to death.

EXERCISE 7

1. 다음 문장을 보기와 같이 같은 뜻이 되도록 다시 고쳐 쓰시오.

1. 'Why don't you go away for a few days?' Jack said to me.
→ Jack suggested that *I go away for a few days.*

2. 'You really must stay a little longer,' she said to me.
→ She insisted that ______________________

3. 'You must pay the rent by Friday,' the landlord said to us.
→ The landlord demanded that ______________________

4. 'I think it would be a good idea to see a specialist,' the doctor said to me.
→ The doctor recommended that ______________________

5. 'Why don't you visit the museum after lunch?' I said to them.
→ I suggested that ______________________

2. 다음 문장을 어법에 맞게 고치시오.

1. It was urgent that he called her immediately.
2. It was very important that we delay discussion.
3. Tom suggested me to look for another job.
4. I advise you take the prerequisites before registering for this course.
5. It is the recommendation of many psychologists that a learner uses mental images to associate words and remember names.
6. Where do you suggest I go for my holiday?
7. What do you think of Jane's insistence that he apologizes.

4 wh-명사절

1. 의문사로 시작되는 wh-명사절은 직접의문문이 간접의문문으로 바뀐 구조로서, 의문사가 접속사 역할을 하여 어순은 「의문사+주어-동사」가 된다. 문장에서 주어, 목적어, 보어로 쓰인다.

(1) Where is he going? + It is a secret.
→ Where he's going is a secret. (주어)

(2) I don't know. + Where does she live?
→ I don't know where she lives. (목적어)

(3) My conclusion was. + Who will take care of the children?
→ My conclusion was who would take care of the children.(보어)

2. what, who 자체가 주어로 사용될 경우, wh-명사절의 어순은 「의문사+동사」가 된다.

(4) What has happened?
→ I wonder what has happened.

Further Study

1. The old woman was deeply moved by what he said and she came to know what his words meant.

2. Scientists still cannot predict exactly when a volcano will erupt or how much damage it will cause.

3. By studying a skeleton, a trained scientist can tell how old the person was at his time of death, and whether that person was male or female.

4. Psychology is concerned with how people think, feel, imagine, hope, and dream, and how those mental activities influence what people say and do.

Exercise 8

1. 다음 직접의문문을 wh-명사절로 바꾸어 문장을 완성하시오.

1. Why did Tom leave?
→ I don't know ______________________________

2. Where is the post office?
→ Could you please tell me ______________________

3. What time is it?
→ Could you please tell me ______________________

4. How can I improve my English?
→ ____________________________ is a serious concern.

5. What country is Anna from?
→ Do you know ______________________________

2. 괄호 안의 단어를 알맞게 고쳐 문장을 완성하시오.

1. A: Where (Ruth, go) __________? She's not in her room.
   B: I don't know. Ask her friend Tina. She might know where (Ruth, go) __________.
2. A: Oops! I made a mistake. Where (my eraser, be) __________? Didn't I lend it to you?
   B: I don't have it. Ask Sally where (it, be) __________. I think I saw her using it.
3. A: The door isn't locked! Why (Fred, lock, not) ______________ it before he left?
   B: Why ask me? How am I supposed to know why (he, lock, not) ______________ it? Maybe he just forgot.
4. A: Mr. Lee is a recent immigrant, isn't he? How long (he, be) ______________ in this country?
   B: I have no idea, but I'll be seeing Mr. Lee this afternoon. Would you like me to ask him how long (he, live) ______________ here?

5 whether/if-명사절

1. yes-no 의문문이 간접의문문으로 바뀐 구조로서, whether나 if가 접속사로 사용되어 어순은 「whether/if+주어-동사」가 된다.

(1) I don't know. + Is Eric at home?
→ I don't know whether/if he is at home. (목적어)

(2) Does she have a car? + It's not important to me.
→ Whether she has a car isn't important to me. (주어)

2. 문장 끝에 or not가 올 수 있다.

(3) Please tell me whether/if Eric is at home (or not).

3. 문장의 주어나 전치사의 목적어로 쓰일 경우 접속사 whether만이 올 수 있다.

(4) Whether/*If she comes or not is another matter.

(5) Mike is really interested in whether/*if God exists (or not).

FURTHER STUDY

1. Because he had an appointment, he asked his boss if he could leave work early.

2. Whether you agree or not doesn't matter as long as you show interest in the conversation.

3. He had trouble finding out whether the capital of the country lay in the coastal area or in the mountain.

4. First, you should check the weekly newspaper ads. Find out the items that are on sale and decide if you really need those things.

EXERCISE 9

1. 다음 의문문을 whether나 if를 사용한 명사절로 바꾸어 문장을 완성하시오.

1. Did Steve go to the bank?
→ I don't know ______________________________
2. Is Karen at home?
→ Do you know ______________________________
3. Is Sydney the capital of Australia?
→ ______________________________ is the first question.
4. Is Pat feeling better today?
→ I wonder ______________________________
5. Is there life on other planets?
→ No one knows ______________________________
6. Can Jane come to the conference?
→ ______________________________ is important to me.
7. Is there a Santa Claus?
→ The little boy wants to know ______________________
8. Are we going to have a test tomorrow?
→ Let's ask the teacher ______________________________

2. 다음 문장을 어법에 맞게 고치시오.

1. I wonder why was Bob late for class.
2. I don't know what does that word mean.
3. Please tell me what is your name.
4. I wonder does the teacher know the answer.
5. I'll ask her that she would like some coffee or not.
6. I wonder does Tom know about the meeting or not.
7. What my friend and I did was our secret. We didn't even tell our parents what did we do.
8. I don't understand why is the car not running properly.

제 9 장

형 용 사 절

1. 형용사절
2. 주격 관계대명사
3. 목적격 관계대명사
4. 소유격 관계대명사
5. 관계대명사 what/which
6. 계속적 용법

1 형용사절

1. 형용사의 주된 기능은 명사의 수식이다. 이러한 형용사의 기능을 가지는 절(節)을 형용사절 혹은 관계절이라 한다.

   i) 형용사: 명사 앞에서 수식

   (1) I met a kind man.

   ii) 형용사절: 명사 뒤에서 수식

   (2) I met a man who is kind.

2. 형용사절을 이끄는 who, which 등을 관계대명사라 하며, 두 문장을 이어주는 접속사와 대명사의 역할을 동시에 가지며 선행사에 따라 달라진다. 문장의 25%가 형용사절을 가질 만큼 관계대명사는 독해에서 중요하다.

   (3) The employees who work in this factory are very diligent.
   (The employees: 선행사, who: 관계대명사)

   (4) I bought the book which you mentioned last week.
   (the book: 선행사, which: 관계대명사)

3. 관계대명사는 형용사절 내에서 가지는 문법적 역할에 따라 주격, 목적격, 소유격이 있다.

   (5) I looked for the man who sent me the bill last week.
   I looked for the man whom Robert had met.
   I looked for the man whose credit card has expired.

   (6) Toronto has a building which is the tallest in the world.
   Toronto has a building which you can get a nice view from.
   Toronto has a building whose view is fantastic.

EXERCISE 10

1. 다음 문장에서 선행사와 형용사절을 찾아 표시하시오.

1. The man [who lives next door] is very friendly.
   선행사 형용사절
2. A burglar is someone who breaks into a house and steals things.
3. We saw some people whose car had broken down.
4. The woman who Jack is going to marry is Japanese.
5. Most beans that are cultivated in the United States are a form of kidney beans.
6. You should not say things that might make a highly sensitive person upset.
7. Jerry works for a company which makes typewriters.
8. A dictionary is a book which gives you the meanings of words.

2. 다음 문장이 올바른지(√), 틀린지(×)를 표시하시오.

1. _×_ We stayed in a hotel who had a beautiful garden.
2. ____ I didn't like the man which my sister married.
3. ____ Did I tell you about the film which we saw?
4. ____ Eric said a word which I couldn't understand it.
5. ____ People that live in London are called 'Londoners.'
6. ____ Is the book you're reading interesting?
7. ____ I'm spending the day with some people I know.
8. ____ The people came to dinner stayed very late.
9. ____ The girl I work with gave me some flowers.
10. ____ I didn't believe anything what she says.

2 주격 관계대명사

1. 관계대명사가 형용사절의 주어 역할을 하면서 선행사가 사림일 때 who나 that을 사용한다.

(1) The man is friendly. [⇓ **who** / **that**] lives next to me.

→ The man *who lives next to me* is friendly.
The man *that lives next to me* is friendly.

2. 관계대명사가 형용사절의 주어 역할을 하면서 선행사가 사물일 때 which나 that을 사용한다.

(2) The river is polluted. It flows through town.
→ The river *which flows through town* is polluted.
The river *that flows through town* is polluted.

3. 주격 관계대명사가 올 때, 형용사절의 동사는 선행사의 수와 일치해야 한다.

(3) I know the man who is sitting over there.
I know the people who are sitting over there.

(4) Korea is a country which is located in the Far East.
Korea and China are countries which are located in the Far East.

EXERCISE 11

1. 문장 b를 형용사절로 하여 주어진 두 문장을 결합하시오

1. a. Do you know the people? b. They live in the white house.

____

2. a. I have a class. b. It begins at 8:00 AM.

____

3. a. The police officer was friendly. b. He gave me directions.

____

4. a. The waitress was friendly. b. She served us dinner.

____

5. a. I know a man. b. He doesn't have to work for a living.

____

2. 다음 둘 중에서 올바른 것을 고르시오.

1. The students who (is/are) in my class come from many countries.
2. The student who (is/are) talking to the teacher is from Peru.
3. I met some people who (knows/know) my brother.
4. Anybody who (has/have) lost his ticket should report to the desk.
5. Do you know the people that (lives/live) in that house?
6. A book that (tells/tell) the story of a person's life is called a biography.
7. There's the man who (took/he took) your coat.
8. Do you know the people who (live/they live) next door?
9. I like that woman; (she is/is) very kind.
10. The car which (is parked/it is parked) outside belongs to Susan.

3 목적격 관계대명사

1. 관계대명사가 형용사절의 목적어 역할을 하면서 선행사가 사람일 때 whom이나 that을 사용하거나 생략할 수 있다.

(1) The man was friendly. I met him.

him. ⇓ **whom** / **that** ↓ ***whom*** *I met*

→ The man *whom I met* was friendly.
The man *that I met* was friendly.
The man *Ø I met* was friendly.

2. 관계대명사가 형용사절의 목적어 역할을 하면서 선행사가 사물일 때 which나 that을 사용하거나 생략할 수 있다.

(2) The books were expensive. I bought them.
→ The books *which I bought* were expensive.
The books *that I bought* were expensive.
The books *Ø I bought* were expensive.

3. 관계대명사가 전치사의 목적어일 때, 전치사는 동사 뒤에나 관계대명사 앞에 올 수 있다. 전치사가 관계대명사 앞에 올 경우 whom/which만이 올 수 있다.

(3) The man was helpful. I talked to him.
→ The man *whom / that / Ø I talked to* was helpful.
The man *to whom I talked* was helpful.

(4) The chair is hard. I am sitting in it.
→ The chair *which / that / Ø I am sitting in* is hard.
The chair *in which I am sitting* is hard.

EXERCISE 12

1. 괄호 안의 문장을 형용사절로 하여 두 문장을 결합하되, 가능한 모든 형태를 쓰시오.

   1. The woman gave me some information. (I called her.)

      ____

   2. All of the people can come. (I asked them to my party.)

      ____

   3. I lost the scarf. (I borrowed it from my roommate.)

      ____

   4. The bus is always crowded. (I take it to school every morning.) ______________________________

   5. The candidate didn't win the election. (I voted for her.)

      ____

   6. I ran into a woman. (I had gone to elementary school with her.) ______________________________

2. 다음 둘 중에서 올바른 것을 고르시오.

   1. I don't understand the theory (that, whom) Steven Hockin produced.
   2. She is the girl about (who, whom) we talked the other day.
   3. The policeman we talked (to, Ø) was very friendly.
   4. I've found the keys which (I lost/I lost them).
   5. Do you like the new dress which (I bought/I bought it) yesterday?
   6. The subject in (which, that) I'm interested is biology.
   7. This is a new kind of knife: (cuts/it cuts) everything.
   8. The poems which Mark (writes/writes them) are very hard to understand.
   9. I have found the book I was looking for (it, Ø).
   10. Electronics is a subject about (which, Ø) I know very little.

4 소유격 관계대명사

1. 관계대명사 whose는 선행사가 사람이거나 사물이며 소유격인 (대)명사 대신에 쓴다. 관계대명사 whose는 생략할 수 없다.

(1) The man called the police. [His car ⇓ **whose car**] was stolen.

→ The man *whose car was stolen* called the police.

(2) I live in a dormitory. [Its residents ⇓ **whose residents**] come from many countries.

→ I live in a dormitory *whose residents come from many countries.*

2. 선행사가 사물일 경우, 관계대명사 whose는 of which로 쓸 수 있다. of which를 쓸 때 명사 앞에는 정관사 the가 온다.

(3) It was a meeting.
I didn't understand the purpose of the meeting.
→ It was a meeting whose purpose I didn't understand.
It was a meeting the purpose of which I didn't understand.

FURTHER STUDY

1. From time to time we must look up words whose meanings we do not know

2. There are many organizations whose sole purpose is to help mentally retarded children.

3. The man of which the red car is parked in front of our house is a prominent physician in this town.

EXERCISE 13

1. 관계대명사 whose를 이용하여 다음 문장을 결합하시오.
   1. The girl is a good friend of mine. I borrowed her camera.

      ____

   2. He's written a book. Its title is *Women's Freedom.*

      ____

   3. I have to call the man. I accidentally picked up his umbrella after the meeting.

      ____

   4. I thanked the woman. I borrowed her dictionary.

      ____

2. 관계대명사를 이용하여 다음 문장을 결합하되, 가능한 모든 형태를 쓰시오.
   1. Mr. North teaches a class for students. Their native language is not English.

      ____

   2. The man poured a glass of water on his face. His beard caught on fire when he lit a cigarette.

      ____

   3. They own an original Picasso painting. The value of the painting is more than a million dollars.

      ____

   4. My country is dependent upon its income from coffee. The price of coffee varies according to fluctuations in the world market.

      ____

   5. The professor has assigned the students a research paper. The purpose of the research paper is to acquaint them with methods of scholarly inquiry.

      ____

5 관계대명사 what/which

1. 관계대명사 what은 그 자체 안에 선행사를 포함하고 있다. '~것'으로 해석하며, the thing(s) that 혹은 anything that와 같은 뜻이다.

   (1) Do you have <u>what</u> (=the things that) you need for your journey?

   (2) <u>What</u> I'm most interested in is your personal reactions.

2. 관계대명사 what은 단어나 구를 강조하기 위해 다음과 같이 사용된다.

   (3) I need a laptop computer.
   → <u>*What*</u> *I need* is a laptop computer.

   (4) You should think about your family.
   → <u>*What*</u> *you should think about* is your family.

   (5) She's looking for a job.
   → <u>*What*</u> *she's looking for* is a job.

3. 지시대명사 this와 that은 앞의 문장 전체를 가리킬 수 있다. 마찬가지로 앞에 나온 문장 전체를 선행사로 할 때 관계대명사 which를 사용하며, which 앞에 콤마를 쓴다.

   (6) Tom was late. <u>That</u> surprised me.
   → Tom was late, <u>which</u> surprised me.

   (7) The elevator is out of order. <u>This</u> is too bad.
   → The elevator is out of order, <u>which</u> is too bad.

EXERCISE 14

1. 밑줄 친 부분을 어법에 맞게 고치시오.

   1. This is the thing what I wanted to buy.
   2. The shop didn't have that I wanted.
   3. It rained all night, that was good for the garden.
   4. My phone is out of order, what is a real nuisance.
   5. The woman talked and talked which made me bored.

2. 빈칸에 that나 what을 넣으시오.

   1. I believe everything ________ she says.
   2. ________ she did surprised everybody.
   3. I can't give you ________ you want.
   4. He said nothing ________ was important.
   5. The only thing ________ I forgot was toothpaste.
   6. Ask Peter – he'll tell you ________ you need to know.
   7. I can't eat ________ I like.

3. 두 번째 문장을 형용사절로 하여 두 문장을 결합하시오.

   1. The student next to me kept cracking his knuckles. That bothered me a lot.
   2. Mrs. Anderson responded to my letter right away. I appreciate that very much.
   3. There's been an accident on Highway 5. That means I'll be late to work this morning.
   4. So she has repaid the money she borrowed from me. I appreciate that.
   5. She has promised herself to be on time to work every day. That is a good idea.

6 계속적 용법

1. 형용사절은 제한적(restrictive) 용법과 계속적(non-restrictive) 용법의 두 가지 용법을 갖는다. 제한적 용법은 선행사의 실체를 확인하기 위해 필요한 정보를 제공하는 반면에, 계속적 용법은 선행사의 실체는 이미 알고 있으면서 추가적인 정보를 제공할 경우에 사용한다. 계속적 용법의 경우에는 선행사와 관계대명사 사이에 콤마가 있다.

    (1) The professor who teaches Chemistry 101 is an excellent lecturer.

    (2) Professor Wilson, who teaches Chemistry 101, is an excellent lecturer.

2. 계속적인 용법으로 사용될 경우, 관계대명사 that는 올 수 없으며 목적격일 경우에도 생략할 수 없다.

    (3) The man *whom* / *that* / *Ø I met* teaches chemistry.

    (4) Mr. Lee, *whom* / **that* / **Ø I met yesterday*, teaches chemistry.

FURTHER STUDY

1. This class, which is a prerequisite for microbiology, is so difficult that I would rather drop it.
2. Major Yuri Gagarin, who was from Russia, became the first human to fly into space.
3. There are thousands of kinds of bacteria, many of which are beneficial.
4. The Franklin Corporation, which I applied for last fall, has decided to hire fewer applicants than they had originally intended.

EXERCISE 15

1. 계속적 용법으로 사용되는 경우에는 콤마를 쓰고, 제한적 용법으로 사용되는 경우에는 관계대명사를 that으로 바꾸시오.

   1. Alan and Jackie who did not come to class yesterday explained their absence to the teacher.
   2. The students who did not come to class yesterday explained their absence to the teacher.
   3. The rice which we had for dinner last night was very good.
   4. Rice which is grown in many countries is a staple food throughout much of the world.

2. 주어진 문장과 같은 뜻을 가진 것을 고르시오.

   1. The teacher thanked the students, who had given her some flowers.
      a. The flowers were from *only some* of the students.
      b. The flowers were from *all* of the students.
   2. The teacher thanked the students who had given her some flowers.
      a. The flowers were from *only some* of the students.
      b. The flowers were from *all* of the students.
   3. There was a terrible flood. The villagers who had received a warning of the impending flood escaped to safety.
      a. *Only some* of the villagers had been warned; only some escaped.
      b. *All* of the villagers had been warned; all escaped.
   4. There was a terrible flood. The villagers, who had received a warning of the impending flood, escaped to safety.
      a. *Only some* of the villagers had been warned; only some escaped.
      b. *All* of the villagers had been warned; all escaped.

EXERCISE 16

1. 다음 문장을 어법에 맞게 고치시오.

1. In our village, there were many people didn't have much money.
2. Almost all of the people appear on television wear makeup.
3. I don't like to spend time with people which loses their temper easily.
4. The boy drew pictures of people at an airport which was waiting for their planes.
5. People who works in the hunger program estimate that 3500 people in the world die from starvation every day of the year.
6. I enjoyed the book that you told me to read it.
7. I still remember the man who he taught me to play the violin when I was a boy.
8. The woman about who I was talking about suddenly walked into the room. I hope she didn't hear me.
9. I met a woman who her husband is a famous lawyer.
10. I wrote a thank-you note to the people who I visited their house on Thanksgiving Day.

2. 빈칸에 알맞은 관계대명사를 넣으시오.

1. People ________ live in New York are called New Yorkers.
2. Tina likes the present ________ I gave her for her birthday.
3. Geroge Washington is the president ________ picture is on a one-dollar bill.
4. I like the people with ________ I work.
5. Do you know the woman ________ Michael is engaged to?
6. The person to ________ you should send your application is the Director of Admissions.

제 10 장

부사절

1. 부사절
2. 시간부사절
3. 원인부사절
4. 조건부사절
5. 양보부사절
6. 목적부사절
7. 결과부사절

1 부사절

1. 부사절은 「접속사+주어-동사」의 형태로 부사 역할을 하며, 접속사의 의미에 따라 시간, 이유, 조건, 양보 등의 부사절로 나눈다. 반면에 부사구는 「전치사+명사」의 형태를 갖는다.

   (1) Because the weather was cold, we stayed home. (부사절)
   (2) Because of the cold weather, we stayed home. (부사구)

2. 부사절은 주절 앞에 오거나 뒤에 나올 수 있다. 부사절이 주절 앞에 올 경우 일반적으로 콤마를 사용한다.

   (3) Because he was sleepy, he went to bed.
   (4) He went to bed because he was sleepy.

EXERCISE 17

1. 괄호 안의 두 접속사 중 적합한 하나를 선택하여 보기와 같이 두 가지 방법으로 결합하시오.

1. I'll see you again. We come back from holiday. (while, after)
   I'll see you again after we come back from holiday.
   After we come back from holiday, I'll see you again.
2. I watched TV. John came home. (if, until)
   ____
   ____
3. I'd like to talk to you. You go home. (before, although)
   ____
   ____
4. I enjoyed the film. The beginning was boring.
   (because, although)
   ____
   ____

2 시간부사절

1. 시간의 접속사

after	when	as soon as	whenever
before	while	the moment	every time
until	as	as long as	by the time
since		once	

2. 시간부사절에서는 미래를 나타내기 위해 현재시제를 사용한다.

(1) A: What time will you phone me tomorrow?
B: I'll phone you when I get home from work.
(*I'll phone you when I will get home from work.)

3. after, before, until, since는 접속사와 전치사의 두 가지 기능을 갖는다.

(2) After school, you should go to the doctor. (전치사)
(3) After school is over, you should go to the doctor. (접속사)

FURTHER STUDY

1. I began to comprehend the nature of the project only after I read his fifty-page report.

2. This time people were standing in line outside movie theaters for weeks before the movie was released.

3. Pompeii was almost forgotten until a local peasant discovered a buried wall while he was digging in a vineyard in 1748.

4. He's put on weight since he gave up smoking.

5. Hundreds of people died when the Yangtze River flooded last year.

6. Our house was burgled while we were away on holiday.

7. Almost as soon as the polls closed on the night of October 7th, the networks announced that he had been elected governor of California.

8. He recognized me the moment he saw me.

9. As long as you live with us, you should share the expense.

10. The moment they felt their lives were being threatened, they forgot the fact that they could not move.

11. Once you have made a promise, you should keep it.

12. Coffee reached England before tea did, but once the English tasted tea, it became a favorite mealtime drink.

13. Once a patent is granted by the Patent Office, it becomes the inventor's property and he or she can keep it, sell it, or assign it.

14. A total lunar eclipse occurs whenever the moon passes through the earths' shadow.

15. Every time Prakash sees a movie made in India, he feels homesick.

16. Every time I saw something cool or ironic or funny, I immediately felt the need to phonecam-blog it.

17. I'm always tired out by the time I get home from work.

18. It's not worth going shopping now. By the time we get to the stores, they'll be closed.

EXERCISE 18

1. 주어진 접속사를 이용하여 다음 문장을 결합하시오.

1. I'll find somewhere to live. Then I'll give you my address.
   ______________________ *when* ______________________
2. I'll do the shopping. Then I'll come straight back home.
   ______________________ *after* ______________________
3. It's going to start raining. Let's go home before that.
   ______________________ *before* ______________________
4. She must apologize to me first. I won't speak to her until that.
   ______________________ *until* ______________________

2. 괄호 안의 동사를 현재와 미래시제로 고쳐 대화를 완성하시오.

A: What about my money?
B: I (send) ____________ the check to you as soon as I (have) ____________ it.
A: Why can't you write me a check now?
B: The manager writes the checks. He's away until Tuesday. I can't do anything until he (get) ____________ back. When he (come) ____________ in on Tuesday morning, I (remind) ____________ him about it. I (make) ____________ sure that he (know) ____________ you want the money immediately. If I (post) ____________ the check first class, you (receive) ____________ it on Wednesday.

3. 밑줄 친 부분을 어법에 맞게 고치시오.

1. <u>While</u> I was fifteen years old, I began to learn how to play the cello.
2. The next time <u>I'll visit</u> Tokyo, I'm going to meet Aki.
3. I lived in Vancouver <u>during</u> two years.
4. I stayed at the hotel <u>for</u> the vacation.

3 원인부사절

1. 원인의 접속사

because as since now (that)

2. as와 since는 화·청자가 이미 알고있는 원인을, because는 미리 알지 못했던 원인을 나타낸다. 따라서 이유를 묻는 why 질문에 대한 대답에는 because를 사용한다.

(1) A: Why did Tom get fired?
B: Because he didn't get along well with his co-workers.

3. now (that)은 '지금 ~라는 이유 때문에'란 뜻으로 현재와 미래 상황의 원인을 나타낸다.

(2) Now (that) I've finally finished the project, I'm going to take a trip.

4. because는 접속사이므로 그 뒤에 「주어+동사」가 오지만, because of와 due to 다음에는 명사(구)가 온다.

(3) Because the weather was terrible, we stayed home.
(4) Because of the terrible weather, we stayed home.
(5) Due to the terrible weather, we stayed home.

FURTHER STUDY

1. Since he has been engaged in the business for the past 10 years, he is quite familiar with the goods the firm exports.
2. Yes, I've decided I should be closer to my parents now that they're getting older, so I'm moving back East.

EXERCISE 19

1. 괄호 안의 접속사를 이용하여 다음 문장을 결합하시오.

1. I changed my hotel. The rooms were dirty. (since)

____

2. I didn't like the film. I walked out of the cinema. (because)

____

3. Many young people move to the cities in search of employment. There are few jobs available in the rural areas. (now that)

____

4. All of the students had done badly on the test. The teacher decided to give it again. (since)

____

2. 괄호 안의 표현을 이용하여 문장을 다시 고치시오.

1. We were late to the meeting <u>due to the heavy traffic</u>. (since)
→ We were late to the meeting ____________________

2. Bill has to do all of the cooking and cleaning <u>because of his wife's illness</u>. (because)
→ Bill has to do all of the cooking and cleaning __________
____

3. I couldn't get to sleep last night <u>because it was noisy in the next apartment</u>. (because of)
→ I couldn't get to sleep last night ____________________

4. <u>Since our parents are generous</u>, all of the children in our family have received the best of everything. (because of)
→ ________________________, all of the children in our family have received the best of everything.

4 조건부사절

1. 조건의 접속사

   if　　　unless　　　in case

2. 시간부사절과 마찬가지로 조건부사절에서도 미래시제 대신에 현재시제를 사용한다.

   (1) If it is hot tomorrow, we'll go swimming.

3. unless는 if~not의 뜻으로 부정어와 함께 사용되지 않는다.

   (2) Unless you have a passport, you can't travel abroad.
   = If you don't have a passport, you can't travel abroad.

4. in case는 '~의 경우에, ~의 경우를 대비하여'의 뜻으로 if와는 다른 의미로 사용된다.

   (3) I'll take an umbrella if it rains.
   (I won't take an umbrella if it doesn't rain.)

   (4) I'll take an umbrella in case it rains.
   (I will take an umbrella whether it rains or not.)

FURTHER STUDY

1. We cannot love other people unless we can love our own flesh and blood.

2. Write your name and address on your book in case you lose it.

3. We've installed a burglar alarm in our office in case somebody breaks in.

4. She has pens and pads at her fingertips just in case a great idea comes over her.

Exercise 20

1. 둘 중에서 알맞은 것을 하나 골라 다음 대화를 완성하시오.

Justin: Have you heard about the pop festival?
Carla: Yes, (it's/it'll be) good if Micromoon are playing. They're a great band.
Debbie: Will you be able to go, Dave?
Dave: If (I ask/I'll ask) my boss, he'll give me some time off work, I expect.
Mike: How are we going to get there?
Justin: Well, if enough people (are going/will go), we can hire a minibus.
Vicky: I won't be going if (it's/it'll be) too expensive.

2. 밑줄 친 부분을 어법에 맞게 고치시오.

1. If I'll become President, I'll work for the poor and the weak.
2. If it be sunny tomorrow, we'll go on a field trip.
3. Unless you don't hurry, you'll miss the plane.
4. We'll buy some more food in case Tom will come.

3. 빈칸에 in case와 if 중 알맞은 것을 골라 넣으시오.

1. We've installed a burglar alarm in our office ____________ somebody breaks in.
2. The alarm will go off ____________ somebody breaks into our office.
3. Go to the lost and found office ____________ you lose your bag.
4. Write your name on your bag ____________ you lose your bag.
5. I arranged for insurance ____________ I needed medical treatment while I was abroad.

5 양보부사절

1. 양보의 접속사

although	though	even though
while	whereas	

2. although, though, even though는 예상하지 못한 결과를 나타낸다. 반면에 because는 예상되는 결과를 나타낸다.

(1) Although the weather was cold, I went swimming.
(= The weather was cold, but I went swimming.)

(2) Because the weather was cold, I didn't go swimming.
(= The weather was cold, so I didn't go swimming.)

3. while과 whereas는 '반면에'의 뜻으로 완전히 다른 반대를 나타낸다.

(3) While some people like black coffee, others like it with cream and sugar.

(4) A box is square, whereas a circle is round.

4. although 등은 접속사이므로 「주어+동사」가 뒤따르나, 전치사 despite와 in spite of 뒤에는 명사(구)가 와야 한다.

(5) Despite / In spite of the heavy traffic, we arrived on time.
= Though the traffic was heavy, we arrived on time.

FURTHER STUDY

1. Clicking Next goes to the next screen, while clicking Back which will appear on other screens goes to the previous screen.

2. He looks about forty, whereas his wife looks about twenty.

EXERCISE 21

1. 접속사 although와 but을 이용하여 다음 문장을 결합하시오.

   1. I felt ill. I went on working.

      ____

      ____

   2. I didn't like her. She was very kind.

      ____

      ____

2. 괄호 안의 표현을 이용하여 주어진 문장을 다시 고쳐 쓰시오.

   1. She went on working although she was ill. (in spite of)

      ____

   2. Although I was thirsty, I didn't drink anything. (despite)

      ____

   3. Despite her dislike for coffee, she drank it to keep herself warm. (although)

      ____

   4. In spite of the high prices, my daughters insist on going to the movies every Saturday. (even though)

      ____

3. although / in spite of, because / because of 중 알맞은 것을 넣어 문장을 완성시키시오.

   1. ______________ it rained a lot, we enjoyed our holiday.
   2. a. ______________ all our careful plans, a lot of things went wrong.
      b. ______________ we had planned everything carefully, a lot of things went wrong.
   3. a. I managed to get to sleep ______________ there was a lot of noise.
      b. I couldn't get to sleep ______________ the noise.

6 목적부사절

1. 목적의 접속사

so that~(can)   in order that~(can)
lest~(should)

2. so that~(can)은 '~하기 위하여'의 뜻으로 in order that~(can)과 같은 뜻이다.

(1) I cashed a check so that I could buy my textbooks.
= I cashed a check in order that I could buy my textbooks.

3. 목적을 나타내기 위해서 일반적으로 부정사를 많이 사용한다.

(2) I cashed a check to buy my textbooks. (= in order to buy, so as to buy)
(3) Photocopiers are used to make copies of a written text or reduce the print.

4. lest~(should)는 '~하지 않기 위하여'의 뜻으로 so that~(can not)와 같은 뜻이다.

(4) Hold my arm lest you should fall.
= Hold my arm so that you can not fall.

FURTHER STUDY

1. When I was a child, I would take a flashlight to bed with me so that I could read comic books without my parents' knowing about it.

2. He turned away sharply so that she could not notice the tears in his eyes.

EXERCISE 22

1. 괄호 안의 단어를 사용하여 두 문장을 결합하시오.

1. Please arrive early. We want to be able to start the meeting on time. (so that)

→ *Please arrive early so that we can start the meeting on time.*

2. I'm learning English. I want to get a better job. (to)

→ *I'm learning English to get a better job.*

3. The man spoke very slowly. He wanted me to understand what he said. (so that)

____

4. I slowed down. I wanted the car behind to be able to overtake. (so that)

____

5. Ann and Larry have a six-year-old child. Tonight they're going to hire a babysitter. They want to be able to go out with some friends. (so that)

____

6. A lot of people were standing in front of me. I stood on tiptoes. I wanted to see the parade better. (to)

____

7. I put the milk in the refrigerator. I wanted to make sure it didn't spoil. (lest)

____

8. I'm going on a diet. I want to lose weight. (to)

____

7 결과부사절

1. 결과의 접속사

(so)~that　　　(such)~that

2. so~that 구문: 형용사나 부사가 온다.

(1) The coffee is so *hot* that I can't drink it.
(2) He walked so *quickly* that I couldn't keep up with him.

3. such~that 구문: 형용사의 수식을 받는 명사구가 온다.

(3) It was such *an interesting book* that he couldn't put it down.
(4) This is such *difficult homework* that I will never finish it.

4. 명사구가 many/much, few/little의 수식을 받으면 so~that을 쓴다.

(5) She made so *many mistakes* that she failed the exam.

FURTHER STUDY

1. He has invested so much money in the project that he cannot abandon it now.

2. There are so many products on the market that it is almost impossible to select the best one.

3. There are such small unmarked streets in this section that I often get lost.

4. The term "aggressive behavior" is used in such different ways that no single definition can possibly cover all of its meanings.

EXERCISE 23

1. so~that와 such~that을 이용하여 다음 두 문장을 결합하시오.

   1. This tea is good. I think I'll have another cup.

      ____

   2. This is good tea. I think I'll have another cup.

      ____

   3. The weather was hot. You could fry an egg on the sidewalk.

      ____

   4. I don't feel like going to work. We're having beautiful weather.

      ____

   5. I've met too many people in the last few days. I can't possibly remember all of their name.

      ____

   6. It took us only ten minutes to get there. There was little traffic.

      ____

   7. Ivan takes everything in life too seriously. He is unable to experience the small joys and pleasures of daily living.

      ____

2. so와 such를 넣어 다음 문장을 완성시키시오.

   1. There were ________ few students registered that the class was cancelled.
   2. We had _________ wonderful memories of that place that we decided to return.
   3. There were _________ many people on the bus that we decided to walk.
   4. Kurt had _________ interesting and creative plans that everyone wanted to work on his committee.

제 11 장

분사구문

1. 분사구문 전환
2. 분사구문의 의미

1 분사구문 전환

1. 현재분사나 과거분사로 시작하면서 「접속사+주어-동사」의 부사절과 동일한 기능을 가진 부사구를 분사구문이라 한다.

(1) As he felt rather ill, Tom declined the invitation. (부사절)

(2) *Feeling* rather ill, Tom declined the invitation. (분사구문)

2. 부사절을 분사구문으로 전환하는 방법은 다음과 같다.

1. 접속사는 일반적으로 생략하나, 혼돈을 피하고 정확한 의미전달을 위해 접속사를 그대로 둘 수 있다.
2. 부사절의 주어가 주절의 주어와 동일할 경우 생략한다.
3. 부사절의 동사는 주절의 시제와 같을 경우 현재분사로 바꾼다.

(3) When I read a book, I found a misprint.
→ Reading a book, I found a misprint.

(4) After they sang two songs, they did a dance.
→ After singing two songs, they did a dance.

3. 부사절을 분사구문으로 전환할 때 주의할 점은 다음과 같다.

3-1. 주절의 주어와 부사절의 주어가 다를 때, 분사구문의 주어를 생략하면 비문이 된다. 이런 경우 주절과 분사구문의 주어를 일치시키도록 해야 한다.

(5) *After spending two hours in the waiting room, the nurse called his name.
→ After spending two hours in the waiting room, he was called by the nurse.

(6) *Using a telescope, the stars could be seen clearly.
→ Using a telescope, I could see the stars clearly.

3-2. 주절의 주어와 다를 경우 분사구문의 주어를 별도로 명시할 수 있는데 이를 독립분사구문이라 한다. 대명사는 독립분사구문의 주어로 올 수 없다.

(7) Because the elevator was out of order, we had to walk to the tenth floor.
→ The elevator being out of order, we had to walk to the tenth floor.

(8) *I visiting him, he was working.
→ When I visited him, he was working.

3-3. 부사절이 주절보다 앞선 시제일 때 완료분사구문 「having+pp」를 사용한다.

(9) After we had finished lunch, we went bowling.
→ Having finished lunch, we went bowling.

3-4. 부사절이 수동태일 경우, 「being+pp」를 쓰거나 being을 생략하고 과거분사만 쓸 수 있다.

(10) Because China is located over a vast area, it has a variety of climates.
→ (Being) Located over a vast area, China has a variety of climates.

3-5. 부사절이 부정문이면 분사구문 앞에 not이나 never를 쓴다.

(11) Because Jack didn't want to hurt her feelings, he didn't tell her the bad news.
→ Not wanting to hurt her feelings, he didn't tell her the bad news.

EXERCISE 24

1. 부사절은 분사구문으로, 분사구문은 부사절로 바꾸시오.

1. You should always pray before you go to bed.

____

2. While she was driving to work, she had an accident.

____

3. Because he has gone to New York, he can't help you right now.

____

4. Because the book was written in English, it was too difficult to children.

____

5. While hiking, we admired the scenery around us.

____

6. Needing some money to buy a book, Kevin cashed a check.

____

7. Not knowing exactly what to do, she asked me about that.

____

8. Written in a hurry, this letter has a lot of mistakes.

____

9. Having seen the movie before, I didn't want to go to the movies.

____

2. 밑줄 친 부분을 어법에 맞게 고치시오.

1. <u>Hoped to finish college</u> in three years, Rachel worked very hard.

2. <u>Shocking with the news</u> she had received, she couldn't speak at all.

3. <u>Using in six continents</u>, English is an official or important language in over eighty countries.
4. <u>Seeing from a distance</u>, it would look like a face.
5. <u>Having never met him before</u>, I didn't recognize him.
6. <u>Being fine</u>, we went on a picnic.
7. The book, <u>reading carefully</u>, will become a real teacher.
8. While traveling in Europe, <u>the social reform movement stirred Jane Addams</u>.

3. 다음 빈칸에 가장 적절한 것을 고르시오.

1. ____________, he washed the cup and put it away.
   (A) Having drank the coffee (B) Drinking the coffee
   (C) After drank the coffee (D) Drunk the coffee

2. ____________, I don't type my papers.
   (A) Because don't have a computer
   (B) Don't have a computer
   (C) Not having a computer
   (D) Having not a computer

3. ____________, the book can be read by children.
   (A) Writing in easy English
   (B) Having writing in easy English
   (C) Being writing in easy English
   (D) Written in easy English

2 분사구문의 의미

1. 분사구문은 부사절과 마찬가지로 시간, 원인, 조건, 양보의 의미를 갖는다.

(1) Reaching the river, we pitched camp for the night. (시간)
(= When we reached the river, we ...)

(2) I kept silent at the meeting, not knowing what to say. (원인)
(= I ... , because I didn't know what to say.)

(3) Turning to the left, you will find a coffee shop. (조건)
(= If you turn to the left, you ...)

(4) Knowing that he is idle, I still like him. (양보)
(= Although I know that he is idle, I ...)

2. 분사구문을 이용하여 동시에 일어나는 동작을 나타낼 수 있다. 동시동작은 「with+명사+분사」구문으로 나타낼 수 있다.

(5) Saying "Good-bye", he went out of the house.
(= He went out of the house as he said "good-bye".)

(6) It was a misty morning with little wind blowing.

(7) She sat down with her legs crossed.

3. 분사구문은 연이어 일어나는 동작이나 결과를 나타낼 수 있다.

(8) The train leaves at 5 o'clock, arriving in Pusan at 10 o'clock.
(= The train leaves at 5 o'clock, and it arrives in Pusan at 10 o'clock.)

(9) The teacher smiled at us, saying that he agreed with Jane.
(= The teacher smiled at us, and said that he agreed with Jane.)

1. While rummaging through some old boxes in the attic, I ran across my grandmother's wedding dress.

2. After becoming a doctor, she returned to the Omaha reservation and traveled great distances to visit her many patients.

3. Always wash your hands before handling food. Thoroughly wash all raw vegetables and fruits to remove dirt, chemicals, and insecticides. Use a cutting board when cutting vegetables and fruits. Don't cut them up in your hands!

4. Having the highest marks in his class, he was offered a scholarship by the college.

5. Compared to monkeys, dogs have a fairly low intelligence.

6. Asked if he could come to the party last night, John nodded his head and left the room

7. Francis Preston Blair, Jr., although born in Kentucky, lived and practiced law in Missouri.

8. Although managed by an independent governor and board of directors, the Bank of Canada is owned by the Canadian government.

9. The airport, while large, lacked many basic conveniences.

TIP

rummage 뒤지다, 샅샅이 찾다; attic 다락방; ran across 우연히 찾아내다; reservation 인디언 보호지역 thoroughly 철저히; raw 생것의, 날것의; dirt 흙; insecticide 살충제; cutting board 도마; fairly 꽤, 상당히; nod 고개를 끄덕이다; practice law 변호사 개업을 하다; governor (은행) 총재; board of directors 이사회; convenience 편의, 편리, (pl) 편의시설

10. Uninhabited and unexplored until recent times, Antarctica has not been ruined.

11. In 1903, Henry Ford started the Ford Motor Company. Using light, strong steel, he built cars everyone could afford to buy.

12. Water continually moves around the Earth's surface, changing from one form to another.

13. My colleague and I are preparing a strategy for entering the Chinese market, taking various complicated factors into consideration.

14. Tibet was an independent country until the Chinese invaded in 1950. Isolated from the rest of the world, its people spoke the Tibetan language and practiced Tibetan Buddhism known as Lamaism.

15. With doctors watching him carefully, Gardner stayed awake for 264 hours and 12 minutes.

16. The horse was so tremendous that it could easily hold 100 Greek soldiers. The wooden animal, with soldiers hidden inside, was placed outside the walls of Troy.

17. He fell asleep with his mouth open.

TIP

uninhabited 사람이 살지 않은; unexplored 아직 탐사되지 않은; Antarctica 남극대륙; surface 표면; strategy 전략; take … into consideration ~을 고려하다; complicated 복잡한; factor 요인; invade 침략하다; isolate 고립시키다, 분리시키다; tremendous 거대한, 엄청난

18. According to one scientific theory, an asteroid collided with the earth millions of years ago, causing great changes in the earth's climate.

19. Earthquake cause great damage. In 1923 an earthquake hit the Tokyo-Yokohama area, killing about 143,000 people. In 1995 another earthquake struck the city of Kobe. More than 5,000 people died.

20. When a person is vaccinated, a mild form of a disease is deliberately introduced into the body, causing the body to develop immunity to the disease.

21. One international dating site, Match.com, has brought together thousands of couples, resulting in 1,400 marriages.

22. Very strong winds and storms can start suddenly. And avalanches of snow and ice often fall down the mountain, burying everything in their path.

23. Sewage from homes and waste from factories and farms is emptied into rivers, making the water unfit to drink and even unable to support fish and other water life.

24. Eugene O'Neill, widely acknowledged as one of the United States's greatest playwrights, was awarded a Nobel Prize in 1936.

TIP

asteroid 소행성; collide 충돌하다(with); vaccinate 백신(예방) 접종을 하다; deliberately 고의로, 일부러; immunity 면역, 면역력; bring together 묶다, 합치다, 맺어주다; result in ~로 귀착하다, 끝나다; avalanche 눈사태, (산)사태; sewage 오수, 생활하수; empty 비우다, ~에 흘러들다; acknowledge 인정하다; playwright 극작가; award 주다, 수여하다

25. Established in 1865, the Freedmen's Bureau aided newly freed Blacks by providing relief work, educational services, and legal counsel.

26. Started in the 1890s, Billboard magazine was originally a trade magazine of the American industry. By the early 1900s it expanded to include lists of the best-selling and most popular items in the entertainment business.

27. Many small businesses, unable to obtain credit from traditional banks, have been forced to turn to non-bank financial institutions.

28. I have made many purchases in the Internet, including lots of CDs and books.

29. The post office said that the package should arrive within five to six days, depending on the weather.

TIP

establish 설립하다; relief work 구호사업; legal counsel 법률적 조언; item 품목; entertainment 연예, 오락; obtain 얻다, 획득하다; credit 신용, (은행의) 대출금, 융자; be forced to ~하지 않을 수 없다; turn to ~에 의존하다; financial institution 금융기관; make a purchase 구매하다

제 12 장

등위접속사와 등위절

1. 등위접속사
2. 상관접속사
3. 병렬구조

1 등위접속사

1. 등위접속사(coordinating conjunctions)는 단어와 구, 절을 대등하게 이어주는 접속사로서, and, but, or 등이 있다. 둘 이상의 문장에서 공통된 부분을 생략한 나머지 부분을 등위접속사를 이용하여 연결한다.

   (1) *Steve* and *Alice* are coming to dinner.
   (← Steve *is coming to dinner.* Alice *is coming to dinner.*)

   (2) Susan *raised her hand* and *snapped her fingers.*

   (3) *The traffic was bad* but *I arrived on time.*

2. 등위접속사가 셋 이상의 요소를 연결할 경우 각 단어 뒤와 접속사 앞에 콤마를 쓴다. 그러나 두 개의 요소를 연결할 경우에는 콤마를 사용하지 않으나, 절과 절을 연결할 때는 쓴다.

   (4) Steve *and* Alice are coming to dinner.

   (5) Steve, Joe, *and* Alice are coming to dinner.

3. 등위접속사 so, for, yet은 단어나 구가 아닌 절을 연결하며 항상 콤마를 쓴다. so는 '따라서(therefore)', for는 '왜냐하면(because)', yet은 '그러나(but)'의 뜻이다.

   (6) I was tired, so I went to bed early.

   (7) John couldn't go to the meeting, for he was too busy.

   (8) She did not study, yet she passed the exam.

EXERCISE 25

1. 등위접속사 and와 콤마를 이용하여 다음 문장을 결합하시오.

   1. She speaks (French German Japanese).

      ____

   2. I've invited (Paul Alexandra Eric Luke).

      ____

   3. She (addressed stamped posted) the letter.

      ____

   4. My company has offices in (London Cairo).

      ____

2. 다음 빈칸에 and, but, or, so, for 중 알맞은 접속사를 넣으시오.

   1. I've studied English for three years, _____ I can't speak English very well.
   2. Would you like some water _____ some coffee?
   3. It began to rain, _____ I closed the door.
   4. It began to rain, _____ I didn't open my umbrella.
   5. I didn't go swimming, _____ it was so cold.
   6. I washed my car, cleaned my clothes, _____ watered flowers in the garden.
   7. The stereo didn't work, _____ my dad took it back to the shop.

3. 밑줄친 부분을 어법에 맞게 고치시오.

   1. I put milk <u>and sugar and</u> lemon in my tea.
   2. He was tired <u>so</u> he went to bed.
   3. <u>For she was afraid of the cat,</u> the girl hid behind her mother.
   4. Quebec is the largest province <u>and</u> Prince Island is the smallest province.

2 상관접속사

1. 상관접속사(paired conjunction)는 두 개 이상의 단어가 함께 쓰이는 접속사이다. 상관접속사에는 「both ... and」, 「either ... or」, 「neither ... nor」, 「not only ... but also」 등이 있다. 이들은 등위접속사와 의미가 비슷하나 강조의 뜻을 갖는다.

부가(additive)	and	both ... and	not only ... but also
양자택일(alternative)	or	either ... or (neither ... nor)	

2. 주어가 상관 접속사로 연결될 경우, 동사와의 수 일치에 주의해야 한다. both A and B의 경우 가산명사이면 복수 취급한다. not only A but also B, either A or B, neither A nor B는 의미상 B를 강조하기 때문에 동사의 수는 B에 의해 결정된다. A as well as B는 A에 따라 동사의 수가 결정된다.

(1) *Both* my mother *and* my sister are here.
(2) *Neither* my mother *nor* my sister is here.
Neither my mother *nor* my sisters are here.
(3) *Not only* my mother *but also* my sister is here.
Not only my mother *but also* my sisters are here.
(4) My sister *as well as* my mother is here.
My sisters *as well as* my mother are here.

3. 「not only ... but also」는 「not merely ... but (also)」로 바꾸어 쓸 수 있다.

(5) Not only James but also Maria is a doctor.
Not merely James but (also) Maria is a doctor.

EXERCISE 26

1. 상관접속사 both ... and; not only ... but also; either ... or; neither ... nor를 이용하여 다음 문장을 결합하시오.

   1. He does not have a pen. He does not have paper.
   2. Ron enjoys horseback riding. Bob enjoys horseback riding.
   3. You can have tea, or you can have coffee.
   4. Arthur is not in class today. Ricardo is not in class today.
   5. Smallpox is a dangerous disease. Malaria is a dangerous disease.
   6. Her roommates don't know where she is. Her brother doesn't know where she is.

2. 밑줄 친 부분을 어법에 맞게 고치시오.

   1. She can speak both English <u>as well as</u> Spanish.
   2. Nobel was not only a great inventor <u>also</u> a big businessman.
   3. We have seen neither Jane <u>or</u> her sister.
   4. Both my sister and I <u>am</u> interested in medical science.
   5. The teacher as well as the students <u>have to</u> go to the museum.
   6. Neither my brother nor I <u>has</u> ever been to Texas.
   7. Not only Kate but also her sisters <u>was</u> shocked to hear the news.

3. 어법상 틀린 부분을 찾아 고치시오.

   1. Either John will call Marry or Bob.
   2. Not only Sue saw the mouse but also the cat.
   3. Both my mother talked to the teacher and my father.
   4. Either Mr. Anderson or Ms. Wiggins are going to teach our class today.
   5. Oxygen is plentiful. Both air contains oxygen and water.

3 문장의 병렬구조

1. 등위접속사로 연결되는 단어, 구, 절은 문법적으로 동등한 형태여야 한다. 이를 문장의 병렬구조(parallel structure)라고 한다.

(1) *The patient's symptoms were *fever, dizziness,* and *his head hurt.*

→ The patient's symptoms were *fever, dizziness,* and *headache.* (명사+명사)

(2) *Jane is *young, enthusiastic,* and *she has talent.*

→ Jane is *young, enthusiastic,* and *talented.* (형용사+형용사)

(3) *I plan *to attend school* and *studying economics.*

→ I plan *to attend school* and *to study economics.* (부정사+부정사)

(4) *I enjoyed *shopping, cooking* and *swim.*

→ I enjoyed *shopping, cooking* and *swimming.* (동명사+동명사)

2. 상관접속사로 연결되는 어구도 병렬구조를 이루어야 한다.

(5) *The exam tested both *listening* and *to read.*

→ The exam tested both *listening* and *reading.*

(6) *Marta excels *in mathematics* as well as *science.*

→ Marta excels *in mathematics* as well as *in science.*

(7) *He is famous as not only *a novelist* but also *musical.*

→ He is famous as not only *a novelist* but also *a musical.*

3. 병렬구조는 불필요한 부분이 반복되지 않도록 생략한다.

sweet apples and (sweet) pears
in Japan, (in) China or (in) Korea

EXERCISE 27

1. 어법상 틀린 부분을 찾아 고치시오.

   1. Marcia is a scholar, an athlete, and artistic.
   2. The farmer plows the fields, plants the seeds, and will harvest the crop.
   3. Collecting stamps, playing chess, and to mount beautiful butterflies are Derrick's hobbies.
   4. Slowly and with care, the museum director removed the Ming vase from the shelf and placed it on the display pedestal.
   5. Abraham Lincoln was a good president and was self-educated, hard-working, and always told the truth.
   6. Ecologists are trying to preserve our environment for future generations by protecting the ozone layer, purifying the air, and have replanted the trees that have been cut down.
   7. Despite America's affluence, many people are without jobs, on welfare, and have a lot of debts.

2. 다음 두 문장을 병렬구조의 한 문장으로 만드시오.

   1. Mary opened the door. Mary greeted her guests.
   2. Alice is kind. Alice is generous. Alice is trustworthy.
   3. He gave her flowers on Sunday. He gave her candy on Monday. He gave her a ring on Tuesday.
   4. While we were in New York, we attended an opera. While we were in New York, we ate at marvelous restaurants. While we were in New York, we visited some old friends.
   5. Please try to speak more loudly. Please try to speak more clearly.
   6. I should have finished my homework. I should have cleaned up my room.

7. He decided to quit school. He decided to go to California. He decided to find a job.
8. I am looking forward to going to Italy. I am looking forward to eating wonderful pasta every day.
9. I have met his mother. I have not met his father.
10. Jake would like to live in Puerto Rico. He would not like to live in Iceland.

부 록

ANSWER KEY

연습문제 정답

Exercise 1 page 15

1
1. strange 2. happy 3. happily 4. violent
5. terrible 6. quickly 7. relaxed 8. bad
9. properly

2
1. tasted awful 2. feel fine
3. smell nice 4. look wet
5. sounded, interesting 6. seemed upset

Exercise 2 page 32

1
1. me to use his car
2. Peter to be quiet for a minute
3. me to leave early
4. her to phone
6. the students to speak slowly and clearly
7. me to apply for the job
8. me to take Biology 109

2
1. The professor allowed Alan to leave early.
   Alan was allowed to leave early.
2. The general ordered the soldiers to surround the enemy.
   The soldiers were ordered to surround the enemy by the general.
3. My friend advised me to get some automobile insurance.
   I was advised to get some automobile insurance by my friend.

Exercise 3 *page 36*

1

1. John should have his car checked.
2. Mary should have her watch repaired.
3. Mike should have his trousers cleaned.
4. Peter should have his hair cut.
5. Helen should have her kitchen window repaired.
6. Tom and Janet should have their new car serviced.

2

1. clean	2. cleaned	3. wash	4. taken
5. filled	6. shortened	7. pulled out	

Exercise 4 *page 57*

1

1. for students to do their homework.
2. for us to hurry
3. for a child to sit still for a long time
4. for my family to eat turkey on Thanksgiving Day
5. for students to budget their time carefully

Exercise 5 *page 85*

1

1. Do you know (that) India has the second largest population in the world?
2. I hope (that) you'll have a wonderful time.
3. Don't throw that plastic bag into the sea! Don't you know (that) plastic trash kills thousands of marine animals every year.
4. I have a test tomorrow. I suppose (that) I should study tonight. but I'd rather go to a movie.
5. It's hard to deny (that) pollution diminish the quality of our lives.
6. World hunger is a serious problem. Do you realize (that) more than half of the people in the world go hungry every day?
7. Right now I'm single. I can't predict my future exactly, but I assume (that) I will get married someday.

8. The critics praised the movie for the acting, writing and direction, but said (that) they do not believe (that) it will win any major awards.

2

1. That smoking can cause cancer
2. It
3. The fact that
4. is
5. that
6. is that you
7. for the fact that
8. the view that women

Exercise 6 *page 87*

1

1. A: Are you sure (that) you'll be on time tomorrow?
   B: Yes, I'm certain (that) I'll be on time tomorrow. It's a picnic day.
2. A: Are you happy (that) the weather is nice today?
   B: I'm lucky (that) it's a sunny day because today is my wedding day.

2

1. (that) I'll pass the final test
2. (that) strong laws are needed to protect the environment
3. (that) Korea will be reunited in the near future
4. (that) we will not have a math test tomorrow
5. (that) there is any life on other planets

3

1. that
2. so
3. so
4. don't think so
5. hope not

Exercise 7 *page 89*

1

1. I go away for a few days
2. I stay a little longer
3. we pay the rent by Friday

4. I see a specialist
5. they visit the museum after lunch

2
1. It was urgent that he call her immediately.
2. (Correct)
3. Tom suggested that I look for another job.
4. I advise that you take the prerequisites before registering for this course. (OR I advise you to take the prerequisites before registering for this course.)
5. It is the recommendation of many psychologists that a learner use mental images to associate words and remember names.
6. Where do you suggest that I go for my holiday?
7. What do you think of Jane's insistence that he apologize.

Exercise 8 page 91

1
1. why Tom left.
2. where the postoffice is
3. what time it is?
4. How I can improve my English
5. what country Anna is from?

2
1. did Ruth go, Ruth went
2. is my eraser, it is
3. didn't Fred lock, he didn't lock
4. has he been, he has lived

Exercise 9 page 93

1
1. if/whether Steve went to the bank.
2. if/whether Karen is at home?
3. Whether Sydney is the capital of Australia
4. if/whether Pat is feeling better today.
5. if/whether there is life on other planets.
6. Whether Jane can come to the conference
7. if/whether there is a Santa Claus.
8. if/whether we are going to have a test tomorrow.

2

1. I wonder why Bob was late for class.
2. I don't know what that word means.
3. Please tell me what your name is.
4. I wonder whether/if the teacher knows the answer.
5. I'll ask her whether/if she would like some coffee or not.
6. I wonder whether/if Tom knows about the meeting or not.
7. What my friend and I did was our secret. We didn't even tell our parents what we did.
8. I don't understand why the car is not running properly.

Exercise 10 — *page 97*

1

1. The man [who lives next door] is very friendly.
2. A burglar is someone [who breaks into a house and steals things].
3. We saw some people [whose car had broken down].
4. The woman [who Jack is going to marry] is Japanese.
5. Most beans [that are cultivated in the United States] are a form of kidney beans.
6. You should not say things [that might make a highly sensitive person upset].
7. Jerry works for a company [which makes typewriters].
8. A dictionary is a book [which gives you the meanings of words].

2

1. ×　2. ×　3. √　4. ×
5. √　6. √　7. √　8. ×
9. √　10. ×

Exercise 11 — *page 99*

1

1. Do you know the people who live in the white house?
2. I have a class which begins at 8:00 AM.
3. The police officer who gave me directions was friendly.
4. a. The waitress who served us dinner was friendly.
5. I know a man who doesn't have to work for a living.

2

1. are　2. is　3. know　4. has
5. live　6. tells　7. took　8. live
9. she is　10. is parked

Exercise 12 page 101

1

1. The woman <u>whom/that/Ø</u> I called gave me some information.
2. All of the people <u>whom/that/Ø</u> I asked to my party can come.
3. I lost the scarf <u>which/that/Ø</u> I borrowed from my roommate.
4. The bus <u>which/that/Ø</u> I take to school every morning is always crowded.
5. The candidate <u>whom/that/Ø</u> I voted for didn't win the election.
   The candidate <u>for whom</u> I voted for didn't win the election.
6. I ran into a woman <u>whom/that/Ø</u> I had gone to elementary school with.
   I ran into a woman <u>with whom</u> I had gone to elementary school.

2

1. that	2. whom	3. to	4. I lost
5. I bought	6. which	7. it cuts	8. writes
9. Ø	10. which		

Exercise 13 page 103

1

1. The girl whose camera I borrowed is a good friend of mine.
2. He's written a book whose title is *Women's Freedom.*
3. I have to call the man whose umbrella I accidentally picked up after the meeting..
4. I thanked the woman whose dictionary I borrowed.

2

1. Mr. North teaches a class for students whose native language is not English.
2. The man whose beard caught on fire when he lit a cigarette poured a glass of water on his face.
3. They own an original Picasso painting the value of which is more than a million dollars.
   They own an original Picasso painting whose value is more than a million dollars.

4. My country is dependent upon its income from coffee the price of which varies according to fluctuations in the world market.
   My country is dependent upon its income from coffee whose price varies according to fluctuations in the world market.
5. The professor has assigned the students a research paper the purpose of which is to acquaint them with methods of scholarly inquiry.
   The professor has assigned the students a research paper whose purpose is to acquaint them with methods of scholarly inquiry.

Exercise 14 *page 105*

1

1. the thing that (OR what)
2. what
3. which
4. which
5. , which

2

1. that
2. what
3. what
4. that
5. that
6. what
7. what

3

1. The student next to me kept cracking his knuckles, which bothered me a lot.
2. Mrs. Anderson responded to my letter right away, which I appreciate very much.
3. There's been an accident on Highway 5, which means I'll be late to work this morning.
4. So she has repaid the money she borrowed from me, which I appreciate.
5. She has promised herself to be on time to work every day, which is a good idea.

Exercise 15 *page 107*

1

1. Alan and Jackie, who did not come to class yesterday explained their absence to the teacher.

2. The students that did not come to class yesterday explained their absence to the teacher.
3. The rice that we had for dinner last night was very good.
4. Rice, which is grown in many countries is a staple food throughout much of the world.

2 1. b 2. a 3. a 4. b

Exercise 16 — *page 108*

1

1. In our village, there were many people <u>who</u> didn't have much money.
2. Almost all of the people <u>who</u> appear on television wear makeup.
3. I don't like to spend time with people <u>who lose</u> their temper easily.
4. The boy drew pictures of people at an airport <u>who were</u> waiting for their planes.
5. People who <u>work</u> in the hunger program estimate that 3500 people in the world die from starvation every day of the year.
6. I enjoyed the book that you told me to read <u>Ø</u>.
7. I still remember the man who <u>Ø</u> taught me to play the violin when I was a boy.
8. The woman about <u>whom</u> I was talking <u>Ø</u> suddenly walked into the room. I hope she didn't hear me.
9. I met a woman <u>whose</u> husband is a famous lawyer.
10. I wrote a thank-you note to the people <u>whose house</u> I visited on Thanksgiving Day.

2

1. who/that 2. which/that/Ø
3. whose 4. whom
5. who/that/Ø 6. whom

Exercise 17 — *page 110*

1

1. I'll see you again after we come back from holiday.
After we come back from holiday, I'll see you again.

2. I watched TV until John came home.
   Until John came home, I watched TV.
3. I'd like to talk to you before you go home.
   Before you go home, I'd like to talk to you.
4. I enjoyed the film although the beginning was boring.
   Although the beginning was boring, I enjoyed the film.

Exercise 18 — *page 113*

1

1. I'll give you my address when I find somewhere to live.
2. I'll come straight back home after I do the shopping.
3. Let's go home before it starts raining.
4. I won't speak to her until she apologizes to me.

2

will send	have	gets	comes
will remind	will make	knows	post
will receive			

3

1. When
2. I visit
3. for
4. during

Exercise 19 — *page 115*

1

1. I changed my hotel since the rooms were dirty.
2. Now that I didn't like the film, I walked out of the cinema.
3. Many young people move to the cities in search of employment as there are few jobs available in the rural areas.
4. Since all of the students had done badly on the test, the teacher decided to give it again.

2

1. since the traffic was heavy
2. because his wife is ill
3. because of the noise in the next apartment
4. because of our parents' generosity

Exercise 20 — *page 117*

1 it'll be I ask are going it's

2 1. become 2. is
3. hurry 4. comes

3 1. in case 2. if
3. if 4. in case
5. in case

Exercise 21 *page 119*

1
1. Although I felt ill, I went on working.
   I felt ill, but I went on working.
2. I didn't like her although she was very kind.
   She was very kind, but I didn't like her.

2
1. She went on working in spite of her illness.
2. Despite my thirst, I didn't drink anything.
3. Although she didn't like coffee, she drank it to keep herself warm.
4. Even though the prices are high, my daughters insist on going to the movies every Saturday.

3
1. Although 2. In spite of, Although
3. although, because of

Exercise 22 *page 121*

1
1. Please arrive early so that we can start the meeting on time.
2. I'm learning English to get a better job.
3. The man spoke very slowly so that I would (could) understand what he said.
4. I slowed down so that the car behind could overtake.
5. Tonight they're going to hire a babysitter so that they can go out with some friends.
6. A lot of people were standing in front of me. I stood on tiptoes to see the parade better.
7. I put the milk in the refrigerator lest it should spoil.
8. I'm going on a diet to lose weight.

Exercise 23 — page 123

1

1. This tea is so good that I think I'll have another cup.
2. This is such good tea that I think I'll have another cup.
3. The weather was so hot that you could fry an egg on the sidewalk.
4. We're having such beautiful weather that I don't feel like going to work.
5. I've met so many people in the last few days that I can't possibly remember all of their name.
6. There was so little traffic that it took us only ren minutes to get there.
7. Ivan takes everything in life so seriously that he is unable to experience the small joys and pleasures of daily living.

2

1. so
2. such
3. so
4. such

Exercise 24 — page 128

1

1. You should always pray before going to bed.
2. While driving to work, she had an accident.
3. Having gone to New York, he can't help you right now.
4. Written in English, the book was too difficult to children.
5. While we were hiking, we admired the scenery around us.
6. Because he needed some money to buy a book, Kevin cashed a check.
7. Because she did not know exactly what to do, she asked me about that.
8. Because it is written in a hurry, this letter has a lot of mistakes.
9. As I had seen the movie before, I didn't want to go to the movies.

2

1. Hoping to finish college
2. Shocked with the news
3. Used in six continents
4. Seen from a distance
5. Never having met him before

6. It being fine
7. Read carefully
8. Jane Addams was stirred by the social reform movement

3 1. B 2. C
3. D

Exercise 25 *page 137*

1 1. She speaks French, German, and Japanese.
2. I've invited Paul, Alexandra, Eric, and Luke.
3. She addressed, stamped, and posted the letter
4. My company has offices in London and Cairo.

2 1. but 2. or 3. so 4. but
5. for 6. and 7. so

3 1. , sugar, and 2. , so
3. Because she was afraid of the cat,
4. , but

Exercise 26 *page 139*

1 1. He does not have neither a pen nor paper.
2. Both Ron and Bob enjoys horseback riding.
3. You can have either tea or coffee.
4. Arthur is not in class today. Ricardo is not in class today.
5. Not only smallpox but also malaria is a dangerous disease.
6. Both her roommates and her brother don't know where she is.

2 1. and 2. but also 3. nor 4. are
5. has to 6. have 7. were

3 1. John will call either Marry or Bob.
2. Sue saw not only the mouse but also the cat.
3. Both my mother and my father talked to the teacher.
4. Either Mr. Anderson or Ms. Wiggins is going to teach our class today.
5. Oxygen is plentiful. Air contains both oxygen and water.

1

1. Marcia is a scholar, an athlete, and an artist. (nouns)
2. The farmer plows the fields, plants the seeds, and harvests the crop. (present tense verbs)
3. Collecting stamps, playing chess, and mounting beautiful butterflies are Derrick's hobbies. (verbs + *-ing* + nouns)
4. Slowly and carefully, the museum director removed the Ming vase from the shelf and placed it on the display pedestal. (adverbs)
5. Abraham Lincoln was a good president -- self-educated, hard working, and honest. (adjectives)
6. Ecologists are trying to preserve our environment for future generations by protecting the ozone layer, purifying the air, and replanting the trees that have been cut down. (verbs + *-ing*)
7. Despite America's affluence, many people are without jobs, on welfare, and in debt. (prepositional phrases)

2

1. Mary opened the door and greeted her guests.
2. Alice is kind, generous, and trustworthy.
3. He gave her flowers on Sunday, candy on Monday, and a ring on Tuesday.
4. While we were in New York, we attended an opera, ate at marvelous restaurants, and visited some old friends.
5. Please try to speak more loudly and clearly.
6. I should have finished my homework, and cleaned up my room.
7. He decided to quit school, to go to California, and to find a job.
8. I am looking forward to going to Italy, and eating wonderful pasta every day.
9. I have met his mother(,) but not his father.
10. Jake would like to live in Puerto Rico(,) but not in Iceland.

【저자약력】

경북대학교 사범대학 영어교육과 졸업

경북대학교 대학원 영어영문학과 졸업 (문학박사)

현재 경일대학교 외국어통역학부 영어전공 교수

<저서>

대학영문법, 시사영어, 영어의 근원과 구조 외 다수

영어 구문의 이해

인쇄 / 2012년 8월 27일
발행 / 2012년 9월 5일

저 자 / 정 무 주
발행인 / 김 창 석
발행처 / 홍 익 출 판 사

대구광역시 중구 삼덕 3가 245-2
(053) 421-6700, 427-3627
등록 1987년 11월 26일 제1-107호

정가 10,000원

ISBN 978-89-7826-203-3 93740